2ND EDITION

PIANO · VOCAL · GUITAR

THE TONY AWARDS® SONGBOOK

The American Theatre Wing's Tony Awards
Presented by the League of American Theatres and Producers
and the American Theatre Wing

www.TonyAwards.com

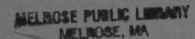

ISBN 978-0-6340-7339-7

7777 W. BLUEMOUND RD. P.O. BOX 13819 MILWAUKEE, WI 53213

Visit Hal Leonard Online at
www.halleonard.com

78211
Tony

CONTENTS

* Though the Tonys were established in 1947, the award for Best Musical did not begin until 1949.

TONY
AWARDS

ALPHABETICAL LISTING
BY SONG TITLE

FOREWORD
BY AUDRA McDONALD

I grew up in Fresno, California, which is a long way from New York City.

To say that I always dreamed of starring in musicals is an understatement. There had been music in my life for as long as I could remember. I sang in the church choir, in school musicals, and even in the local dinner theatre, but what I wanted to do more than anything was perform on Broadway.

And yes, I practiced Tony Award acceptance speeches in my bathroom mirror as a child.

After high school I came to New York to study at the Juilliard School. While my classical training has proved invaluable, musicals can be a different animal altogether. The performance becomes more about the story, the emotion, and the drama of the specific moment and less about perfect technique and purity of sound. Performing in a musical scared and thrilled me at the same time, like a roller coaster ride. It still does.

The shows for which I received Tony nominations and awards are a part of a tradition exemplified by many of the songs in this book. Broadway has so often extolled musicals with a social consciousness, as well as shows that test the very limits of the art form. These shows educate, enlighten as they entertain. They lift up the soul.

Winning a Tony Award is an incredible, almost out-of-body experience. But there is something more magical, and that is what you experience in theatre eight times a week: the amazing connection between the audience and the performer, the intoxicating electricity in the air during those glorious moments that make live theatre so special. Believe me, there is nothing better.

In that spirit I am thrilled to introduce this collection of songs from Tony Award-winning Best Musicals. These songs are treasures, but not just on the printed page. They are meant to be performed. So turn the pages and sing, sing, sing!

Audra McDonald has received Tony Awards for her performances in *Carousel* (1994), *Master Class* (1996) and *Ragtime* (1998). In 2000 she was nominated again for her performance in *Marie Christine*. She has recorded three solo albums, performed in film and on television, and made numerous concert appearances across the U.S.

INTRODUCTION
BY TED CHAPIN

This collection of songs from musicals that have won the Tony Award for Best Musical provides an interesting and even surprising history of the evolution of Broadway over the last 50-plus years.

You'll find some old favorites, some overlooked gems, and some fascinating discoveries. What is Broadway if not songs like "Memory," "Some Enchanted Evening," "The Impossible Dream," "Hello, Dolly!," "Tomorrow," and "Send in the Clowns"? They're all here. But when you look at an index that includes "Mama, Look Sharp" from *1776*, "Look Who's in Love" from *Redhead*, "Measure the Valleys" from *Raisin*, and "Mr. Monotony" from *Jerome Robbins' Broadway*, you may well be surprised by some of the shows that were voted Best Musical each year since 1949. There were some extraordinary seasons in which all nominees felt like winners—1960, for example, when *Gypsy, Once Upon a Mattress* and *Take Me Along* competed with *Fiorello!* and *The Sound of Music*, which tied for the top prize.

One of the joys and pleasures of the Broadway musical has been its diversity. No two shows represented in this collection are the same, and no two songs are the same. The range includes love ballads, anthems, showy arias, haunting odes—even comedy songs—and they're all singable. Variety is the lifeblood of Broadway, and variety is what this collection has in abundance. These songs sing well of the excellence that the Tony Awards have always represented, and will continue to represent.

Ted Chapin, President of The Rodgers & Hammerstein Organization, serves on the Board of the American Theatre Wing, and is also a member of the Tony Awards Administration and Management Committees. He is author of *Everything Was Possible: The Birth of the Musical "Follies"* (Alfred A. Knopf).

A Brief History of the Tony Awards

The American theatre's most coveted award, the American Theatre Wing's Antoinette Perry "Tony" Awards celebrate "distinguished achievement" on stage and behind the scenes. They honor artists and productions in 22 competitive categories, covering plays, musicals, and non-traditional theatrical events. The Tonys also recognize other worthy individuals and organizations through a variety of special awards.

THE KING OF BROADWAY

The Producers, the new Mel Brooks musical (2001) is the most nominated musical in Tony history, with 15. It also holds the record as the musical that won the most Tonys, triumphing in 12 categories, including Best Musical. The three awards it didn't win were due to its multiple nominations in acting categories.

Thanks to a unique marriage between theatre and television, millions of theatre fans watch nominated performances in their own living rooms each June. It's been said that Tony night is the evening when America watches Broadway. It is also the night when America sings along with Broadway. The general public gets to see, often for the first time, many of the production numbers that await them in the playhouses of the Big Apple, some of which will soon travel to their hometown on national tour. And to hear the show tunes of today that—who knows?—might just become the standards of tomorrow.

l to r: Presenter Helen Hayes poses with winners Yul Brynner, Gertrude Lawrence, Phil Silvers and Judy Garland (1952).

Photo: Harry Ransom Humanities Research Center The University of Texas at Austin

The Early Years

The Tonys got their start in 1947 when the American Theatre Wing established an awards program to celebrate excellence in the theatre.

l to r: Winners Mary Martin, Jackie Gleason, Anne Bancroft and Melvyn Douglas (1960)

Photo: Harry Ransom Humanities Research Center The University of Texas at Austin

Named for Antoinette Perry, an actress, director, producer, and the dynamic wartime leader of the American Theatre Wing who had recently passed away, the Tony Awards made their official debut at a dinner in the Grand Ballroom of the Waldorf Astoria hotel on Easter Sunday, April 6, 1947. Vera Allen, Perry's successor as chairwoman of the Wing, presided over an evening that included dining, dancing, and a program of entertainment. The dress code was black tie optional, and the performers who took to the stage included Mickey Rooney, Herb Shriner, Ethel Waters, and David Wayne. Eleven Tonys were presented in seven categories, and there were eight special awards, including one for Vincent Sardi, proprietor of the eponymous eatery on West 44th Street. Big winners that night included José Ferrer, Arthur Miller, Helen Hayes, Ingrid Bergman, Patricia Neal, Elia Kazan and Agnes de Mille.

From the very first year, the Broadway community embraced the Tonys. What began as a modest event grew into an annual celebration of theatrical achievement. But for their first two decades, the Tonys were a much more intimate affair than they are today.

Winners Zero Mostel and Liza Minnelli have fun backstage at the 1965 Tony Awards.

Photo: Photofest

Each year from 1947 until 1965, the dinner and Tony Awards presentation were held in ballrooms of such hotels as the Plaza, the Waldorf Astoria, and the Hotel Astor. The ceremonies were broadcast over WOR radio and the

Presenter Barbra Streisand poses backstage with the winners of the 1967 Tony Award for Best Musical (*Cabaret*): Joe Masteroff, John Kander, Fred Ebb and Harold Prince.

Photo: Copyright 2004 ABC Photography Archives

Mutual network, and in 1956, televised locally for the first time on Du Mont's Channel 5. Entertainment was provided by such Broadway favorites and talented then-newcomers as Katherine Cornell, Guthrie McClintic, Ralph Bellamy, Joan Crawford, Alfred de Liagre, Jr., Gilbert Miller, Shirley Booth, Carol Channing, Joan Fontaine, Paul Newman, Geraldine Page, Anne Bancroft, Sidney Poitier, Fredric March, Robert Goulet, Gig Young, Anna Maria Alberghetti, Henry Fonda, and many others.

THE PRINCE OF BROADWAY

Harold Prince has earned more Tony Awards than anyone else (20 awards), including eight for directing, eight for producing, two as producer of the year's Best Musical, and two special Tony Awards.

In spite of the untimely death of Helen Menken, then chairwoman of the Wing, the 1966 Tony Awards were presented at the Rainbow Room. The ceremony was subdued, and for the first and only time, held in the afternoon without entertainment. The following year the Tony ceremony was once again a gala affair, but with a key difference. With Isabelle Stevenson as its new president, the Wing invited The League of American Theatres and Producers, Inc. (then known as the League of New York Theatres) to co-present the Tonys in 1967, just in time for the ceremony's inaugural broadcast on network television. For the first time, a national audience could watch the presentation of Tony Awards.

NOW AND FOREVER

The Best Musical with the longest Broadway run to date is *Cats*, which played 7,485 performances at the Winter Garden Theatre.

l to r: Lena Horne, Elizabeth Taylor, Ben Vereen (1981)

Photo Courtesy of Alexander H. Cohen

The Television Era

l to r: Presenters Carol Channing, Jerry Herman and Colleen Dewhurst share a laugh with hostess Angela Lansbury (middle) at the 1989 Tony Awards.

Photos by Anita & Steve Shevett

Mikhail Baryshnikov (left), Tony nominee for Best Actor in *Metamorphosis*, congratulates Jerome Robbins, winner as Best Director of a Musical for *Jerome Robbins' Broadway* (1989).

Alexander H. Cohen produced the historic broadcast, which lasted only an hour, and organized a celebratory gala that followed immediately afterward. That year the Tonys moved from their traditional hotel ballroom setting to a Broadway theatre—the Shubert. Cohen continued to produce the awards ceremony and the gala dinner for the next two decades, overseeing their national telecast on various networks on behalf of the League and the Wing. During his tenure, the Tonys became known as the finest awards program on television, incorporating live performances with the bestowal of actual awards. The Cohen era ended in 1987, and that year the Wing and the League created Tony Award Productions, a joint venture that has continued to produce the awards and their related events to this day.

THE HOSTESS WITH THE MOSTES'

Angela Lansbury has hosted or co-hosted more Tony telecasts than any other individual, with five telecasts (1968, 1971, 1987, 1988, and 1989). Tied in second place, with three telecasts each, are Julie Andrews (1970, 1984, and 1991), Robert Preston (1967, 1974, and 1984), and Rosie O'Donnell (1997, 1998, and 2000).

CBS began carrying the broadcast in 1978 and has aired the Tonys every year since. For six years, beginning with the 51st annual awards presentation in 1997, the Tony Awards program took on a new format, thanks to a unique partnership between CBS and PBS. The result was a one-hour PBS special that covered ten awards, immediately preceding the CBS broadcast. However, beginning in 2003, CBS devoted an entire three-hour time slot to the Tonys. The result was a seamless awards and entertainment program on that network.

Harvey Fierstein (2003)

l to r: Donna Murphy, Nathan Lane, Zoe Caldwell, George Grizzard (1996)

The Tonys celebrated a milestone in 1997 when the awards ceremony moved away from Broadway for the first time in 30 years. The switch to New York's celebrated Radio City Music Hall allowed the Tonys to invite members of the general public to attend the awards at this historic, nearly 6000-seat facility, which can also accommodate cast and crew members of all nominated shows. With the exception of 1999, when the Tonys returned to a Broadway theatre (the Gershwin) in order to accommodate renovations at the Music Hall, the Tonys have been held at Radio City ever since.

Gregory Hines and Agnes de Mille, watched over by giant Hirschfeld drawings of Rodgers and Hammerstein (1993)

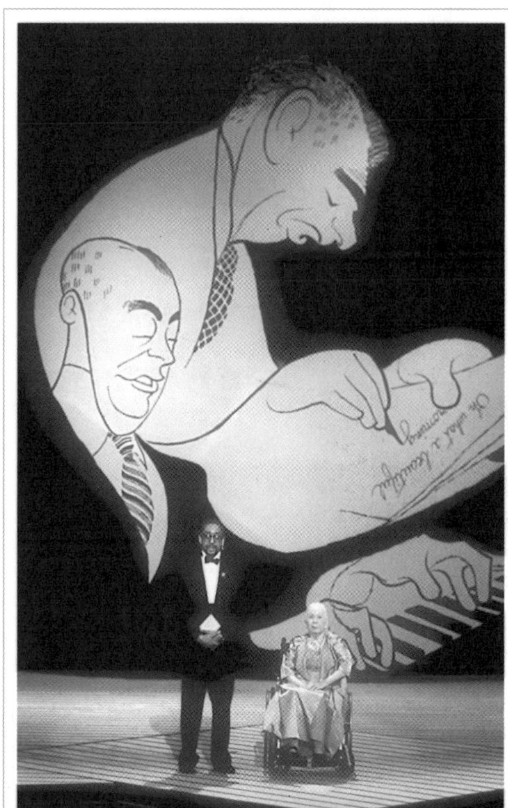
Hirschfeld drawings © Al Hirschfeld / Margo Feiden Galleries Ltd, New York. www.AlHirschfeld.com

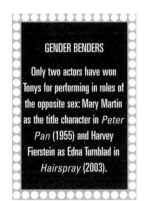

GENDER BENDERS

Only two actors have won Tonys for performing in roles of the opposite sex: Mary Martin as the title character in *Peter Pan* (1955) and Harvey Fierstein as Edna Turnblad in *Hairspray* (2003).

In 1998 IBM joined with the Tonys to launch a website that immediately became the definitive resource for information about the awards. TonyAwards.com serves as a year-round home for the Tonys on the Internet, providing extensive multi-media coverage of the awards and a comprehensive database of past winners and nominees. Among the site's most popular features are video highlights of nominated shows, interviews with nominees, news and feature stories, and a library of videotaped "Tony Memory" interviews with past winners.

Matthew Broderick, presenter (2000)

James Naughton and Julie Andrews (1997)

l to r: Winners Ron Leibman, Madeline Kahn, Chita Rivera and Brent Carver (1993)

All photos on this page by Anita & Steve Shevett

Antoinette Perry (1888–1946)

The Awards' Namesake

When Antoinette Perry died in 1946 at the age of 58, many people who knew her were determined that this remarkable woman of the theatre would not be forgotten.

Born in Denver, Colorado in 1888, Perry made her first impact on the theatre in 1906, when she was only eighteen. She played opposite David Warfield in *Music Master*, and the following year, in David Belasco's *A Grand Army Man*. Only two years later, at an age when most actresses are still waiting for that first big break, Perry retired, a star, to marry and raise a family.

In 1922, after the death of her husband, Frank Freuauff, Perry returned to the stage. She appeared in many plays, including *Minick*, by George S. Kaufman and Edna Ferber, in 1924, and Margaret Anglin's 1927 production of *Electra*. In association with Brock Pemberton, she then turned her talent to directing, enriching the theatre with several memorable plays, including Preston Sturges' comedy *Strictly Dishonorable* in 1929 and Mary Chase's *Harvey* in 1944. *Harvey* was a giant hit, but Ms. Perry died during its Broadway run.

In addition to her career as a director and performer, Perry's off-stage legacy was considerable. This dynamic woman was instrumental in establishing and operating the famed Stage Door Canteen for American soldiers during World War I. As chairman of the board and secretary of the Wing throughout World War II, her dedication and tireless efforts to broaden the scope of theatre through the many programs of the Wing affected thousands of people.

After her death, Jacob Wilk, a story editor at Warner Brothers, first suggested the idea of an Antoinette Perry memorial to producer John Golden. He, in turn, presented the idea to the Wing. Brock Pemberton, a long-time personal friend as well as business associate, was appointed chairman of a commemorative committee, and suggested that the Wing give a series of annual awards in her name. A panel of six Wing members was appointed to nominate candidates for the award in each category. Thus the Tony Awards were born.

SEND IN THE TONYS

Stephen Sondheim has won more Tony Awards than any other composer, with seven: Best Music and Best Lyrics for *Company* (1971); and Best Score for *Follies* (1972), *A Little Night Music* (1973), *Sweeney Todd* (1979), *Into the Woods* (1988) and *Passion* (1994).

MR. VERSATILITY

Michael Blakemore is the only director to win Tony Awards as Best Director of a Play and Best Director of a Musical in the same year. He won for *Copenhagen* (play) and *Kiss Me, Kate* (musical) in 2000.

The Medallion

During the first two years of the Tonys (1947 and 1948), there was no official Tony Award. The winners were presented with a scroll and, in addition, a cigarette lighter (for the men) or a compact (for the women).

In 1949 the designers' union, United Scenic Artists, sponsored a contest for a suitable model for the award. The winning entry, a disk-shaped medallion designed by Herman Rosse, depicted the masks of comedy and tragedy on one side and the profile of Antoinette Perry on the other. The medallion was initiated that year at the third annual dinner. It continues to be the official Tony Award.

Since 1968 the medallion has been mounted on a black pedestal with a curved armature. After the ceremony, each award is numbered for tracking purposes and engraved with the winner's name.

TRIPLE CROWN

Bob Fosse was the only director to win a Tony, an Oscar, and an Emmy in the same year (1973). He won two Tonys (direction and choreography) for *Pippin*, an Oscar for *Cabaret* and an Emmy for "Liza with a Z."

Categories

There are currently 22 competitive categories of Tony Awards, as well as three varieties of special honors that the Tony Awards Administration Committee may bestow on deserving individuals or institutions.

Best Play

Best Musical

Best Revival of a Play

Best Revival of a Musical

Best Special Theatrical Event

Best Score of a Musical Written for the Theatre

Best Book of a Musical

Best Director of a Musical

Best Director of a Play

Best Choreography

Best Set Design

Best Costume Design

Best Lighting Design

Best Orchestrations

Best Performance by a Leading Actor in a Play

Best Performance by a Leading Actress in a Play

Best Performance by a Leading Actor in a Musical

Best Performance by a Leading Actress in a Musical

Best Performance by a Featured Actor in a Play

Best Performance by a Featured Actress in a Play

Best Performance by a Featured Actor in a Musical

Best Performance by a Featured Actress in a Musical

Regional Theatre Tony Award

Special Tony Award for Lifetime Achievement in the Theatre

Tony Honors for Excellence in the Theatre

Though they have represented the pinnacle of theatrical excellence since their inception, the Tonys have evolved in number and designation over the years. For example, although the awards were established in 1947, there was no Tony for Best Play until the following year when *Mister Roberts* by Thomas Heggen and Joshua Logan was so honored. Similarly, the first Best Musical award had to wait two years to make its debut. *Kiss, Me Kate* was the first musical to receive that award, in 1949. The award for Best Special Theatrical Event dates only to 2002.

The Best Musical award has changed over time. During the 1950s and '60s, the award was sometimes shared by a production's authors and its producers. Separate awards were established in 1971, with the producer(s) alone eligible in the Best Musical category. That year saw the debut of the Best Book Award, which recognizes the contribution of the librettist; the composer and lyricist were recognized in their own categories. In fact, 1971 was the only year in which there were separate awards for Best Music and Best Lyrics. Stephen Sondheim won both, for *Company*. The two categories were combined the following year as Best Score of a Musical Written for the Theatre, an arrangement that remains in place today.

Each year since 1976, the Tonys have bestowed a Regional Theatre award on a not-for-profit producing organization outside of New York City, based on the recommendation of the American Theatre Critics Association. Special Tony Awards for lifetime achievement in the theatre recognize an individual for the body of his or her work, and Tony Honors for Excellence in the Theatre recognize the achievements of individuals and organizations that do not fit into any of the 22 competitive categories. In 2003, Tony Honors were bestowed at a separate ceremony held in a Broadway theatre in the autumn, beginning an annual tradition that affords Tony Honors recipients a special moment in the spotlight.

Adapted, in part, from *The Tony® Award: A complete listing with a history of the American Theatre Wing*, edited by Isabelle Stevenson and Roy Somlyo.

Isabelle Stevenson
(1913–2003)

Photo by Anita & Steve Shevett

This songbook is dedicated to Isabelle Stevenson, longtime President and later Chairman of the American Theatre Wing, and the life-force behind the Wing and the Tony Awards for nearly 50 years. Her tireless dedication to the encouragement and recognition of excellence in the American theatre made her a visionary leader of the Wing, creating programs that communicated her own enthusiasm to students, aspiring professionals and general audiences alike. A fixture at opening nights—and on annual Tony telecasts—she lived for, and embodied, the excitement and vitality that theatre offers to us all. Isabelle encouraged the creation of this Tony Songbook, and although she did not have the opportunity to hold it in her hands, we hope she would have been pleased with the results.

The Organizations Behind the Tony Awards

American Theatre Wing

The American Theatre Wing has been an integral and influential part of the theatrical community for the better part of seven decades. Adapting its activities for each successive theatrical generation, ATW focuses today on programs that help students, audiences and theatre professionals to learn more about what makes theatre tick – through the words of the people who make it so vital. Best known for creating The Tony Awards, ATW's reach extends beyond Broadway and beyond New York, with educational and media work that offers the very best in theatre to people around the world. Its television program "Working in the Theatre" and its radio show "Downstage Center" offer sustained conversations with theatre artists, while the Theatre Intern Group and SpringboardNYC offer aspiring professionals early access and insight into theatre as a career. Hundreds of hours of free online media, as well as more information on the work and history of the Wing, is available from www.americantheatrewing.org.

The League of American Theatres and Producers, Inc.

The League of American Theatres and Producers, Inc., founded in 1930 and operating under the trademark "Live Broadway," is the national trade association for the Broadway industry. Its overall goals are to foster increased awareness of and interest in Broadway theatre, and to support the creation of more profitable theatrical productions. The League's 500-plus members include theatre owners and operators, producers, presenters, and general managers in over 140 North American cities, as well as suppliers of goods and services to the theatre industry. Each year, League members bring Broadway to more than 25 million people in New York and on tour across the U.S. and Canada. For more information about League programs and Broadway shows in New York and on national tour, visit www.LiveBroadway.com.

SO IN LOVE
from KISS ME, KATE

Words and Music by
COLE PORTER

E♭ E♭7♭9 A♭ A♭7
the stars fill the sky, so in
D♭ G7 C C7♭9
love with you am I.
poco marc.
Fm C7 Fm
E - ven with - out you, my arms fold
p
B♭m E♭ D♭/F
a - bout you, you know, dar - ling,

D♭m/E
A♭/E♭
E♭7
A♭
why, so in love with you am I.
mf
D♭/A♭
E♭7/A♭
A♭
In love with the night mys - te - ri - ous, the
mf più espressivo
D♭/A♭
E♭7/A♭
A♭
D♭/A♭
night when you first were there, in love with my
cresc. più espr.
E♭7/A♭
A♭
C7/E
Fm
Fm7/E♭
Dm7/♭5
G7
joy de - lir - i - ous when I knew that you could

C
C7♭9
Fm
care. So taunt me and
poco marc.
p
C7
Fm
B♭m
hurt me, de - ceive me, de - sert me.
cresc.
3
E♭
E♭7/D♭
Cm7♭5
F7
I'm yours 'til I die, so in
f passionately
3
B♭m
B♭m7♭5
A♭/E♭
A♭m/E♭
love, so in love, so in

A♭dim/E♭
B♭m7/E♭
E♭7
love with you, my love, am
dim.
1
A♭
C7/G
I.
f
2
A♭
I.
f
poco allarg.
Ped.
p

SOME ENCHANTED EVENING

from SOUTH PACIFIC

Lyrics by OSCAR HAMMERSTEIN II
Music by RICHARD RODGERS

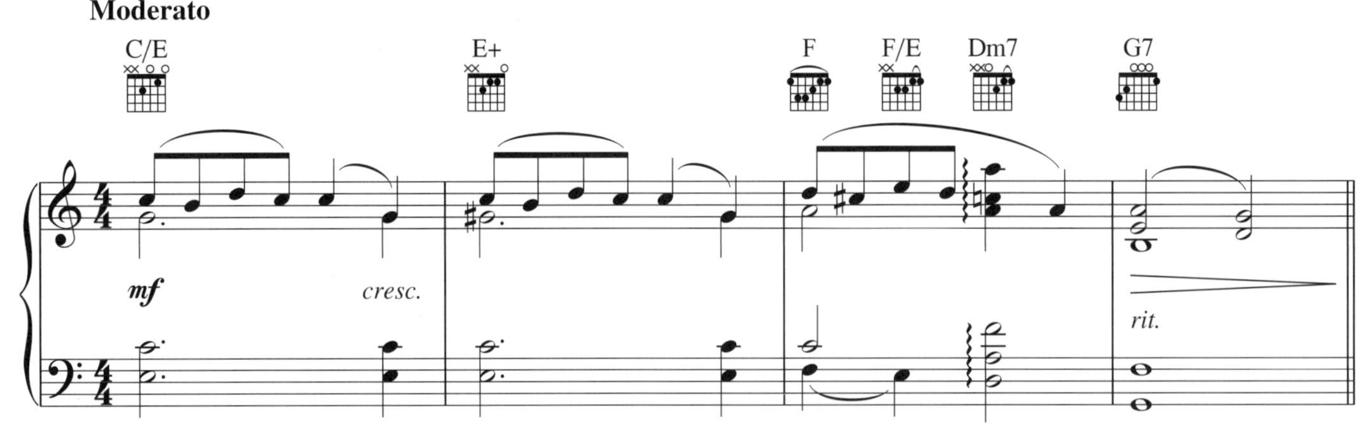

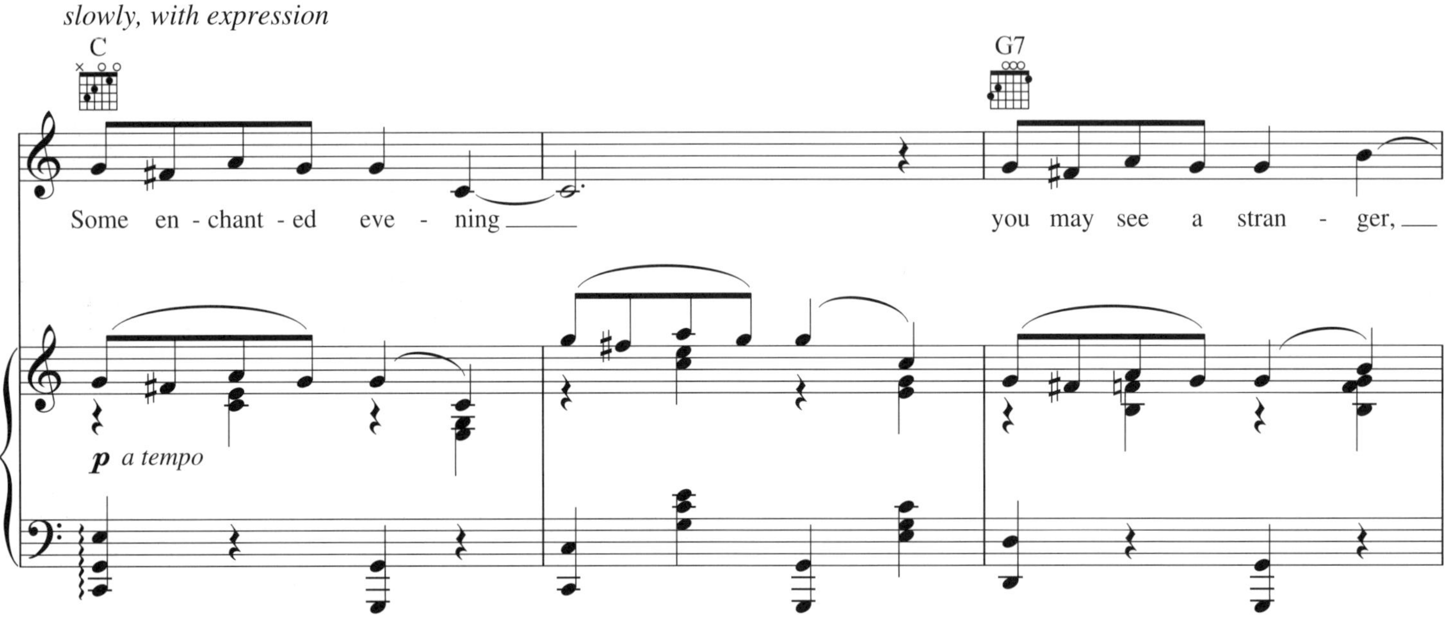

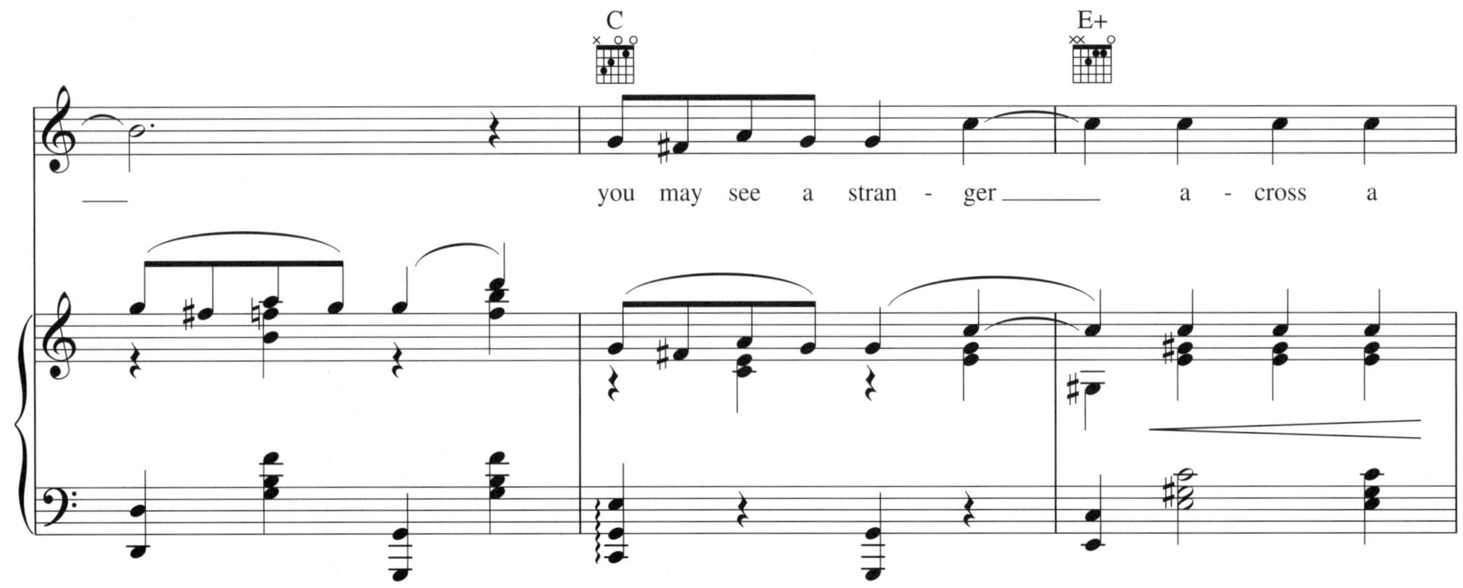

Fmaj7
F6
C6/E
Dm7
G7
Dm
E7
crowd - ed room. And some-how you know, you know e - ven
Am
C7/G
F
C/E
Dm7
G7
then that some-where you'll see her a - gain and a -
mf
Cmaj7
C7
C+
Cdim7/G
4fr
C
gain. Some en - chant - ed eve - ning
p
G7
some - one may be laugh - ing,

C E+ Fmaj7 F6
you may hear her laugh - ing a - cross a crowd - ed room.
C6/E Dm7 G7 Dm E7 Am C7/G
And night af - ter night, as strange as it seems,
F C/E Dm7 G7 C
the sound of her laugh - ter will sing in your dreams.
mf
G7sus G7 Cmaj9 C Dm7 G7 C6 C
Who can ex - plain it? Who can tell you why?
pp

G7sus
G7
Cmaj9
C
Am7
D7
G
Cm6
3fr
Fools give you rea - sons, wise men nev - er try.
cresc. molto
Edim7
Dm7/G
Cdim7/G
4fr
C
Some en - chant - ed eve - ning
mp
Dm7
G7
C
when you find your true love,
when you feel her call you
E+
Fmaj7
F6
C6/E
a - cross a crowd - ed room,
then fly to her
3
mf

Dm7
G7
E7
Am
C7/G
F
C/E
side and make her your own, or all through your
molto espr.
Dm
Dm/G
G7
C
life you may dream all a - lone.
rit.
a tempo
dim.
G7sus
G7
Cmaj9
C
Dm7
G7
C6
C
G7sus
G7
Cmaj9
C
Once you have found her, nev - er let her go. Once you have found her,
pp
Dm/G
C
nev - er let her go!
rit.
mf

IF I WERE A BELL

from GUYS AND DOLLS

By FRANK LOESSER

Medium Bounce (♫ = ♩♪ triplet)

Fmaj7 Dm7 B♭maj7 Gm7 Dm7/C G7♭9/C C13

L.H.

f

A7/E E♭dim7 G9 C13 C13♭9

Ask me how do I feel, ask me now that we're co - zy and
how do I feel, from this chem - is - try les - son I'm

mf - f

F6 C(add9)/E Fm6 F♯dim7

cling - ing. Well, sir, all I can say is if I
learn - ing. Well, sir, all I can say is if I

E♭7 D7 G9 Gm7♭5/D♭ C7 C7♭9

were a bell I'd be ring - ing. From the
were a bridge I'd be burn - ing. Yes, I

F
F/E♭
B♭/D
B♭m/D♭
C7♭9
mo - ment we kissed to - night
that's the way I've just got to be - have.
Boy, if
knew my mo - rale would crack
from the won - der - ful way that you looked.
Boy, if
F6
B♭9
A
B♭7
I were a lamp I'd light,
Or if I were a ban - ner I'd wave.
I were a duck I'd quack,
Or if I were a goose I'd be cooked.
A7/E
E♭dim
G9
C13
C13♭9
6fr
9fr
2fr
3fr
Ask me how do I feel, lit - tle me with my qui - et up -
Ask me how do I feel, ask me now that we're fond - ly ca -
C(add9)/E
Fm6
F♯dim7
bring - ing.
Well, sir, all I can say is if I
ress - ing.
Pal, if I were a sal - ad I know

Eb7 D7 G9 Gm7b5/Db C7 C7b9
9fr
3fr
were a gate I'd be swing - ing. And if
I'd be splash - ing my dress - ing. Or if
F F/Eb Bb/D Abdim7 F/A E7#5
I were a watch I'd start pop - ping my spring,
I were a sea - son I'd sure - ly be spring,
Eb7 D9 D7b9 Dm7/G G9b5 Fmaj7 Dm7 Bbmaj7 C9
4fr
4fr
Or if I were a bell I'd go ding dong ding dong
Or if I were a bell I'd go ding dong ding dong
1
2
F6/9 Abdim Gm9 A7/E Ebdim F6/9 Eb6/9 F6/9
3fr
3fr
6fr
5fr
ding. Ask me ding.
ff

HELLO, YOUNG LOVERS

from THE KING AND I

Lyrics by OSCAR HAMMERSTEIN II
Music by RICHARD RODGERS

A
D/F♯
Fdim7
will.
There are new lov - ers now on the
mf
mp
A7/E
E♭7♭5
D
Dm6
same si - lent hill, look - ing on the same blue sea. And I
A
Dm
know Tom and I are a part of them all, and they're all a part of Tom
G7
Gracefully
C
C6
Cmaj7
C6
and me. Hel -
rit.
mf a tempo

C(add9)
C
Cmaj7
C6
lo, young lov - ers, who - ev - er you are, I
Cmaj7
C6
G7/B
Fm/C
hope your trou - bles are few.
All my good
G7/B
E♭/B♭
6fr
G7/B
Dm7
Dm7/G
G7
wish - es go with you to - night—
I've been in love like
C
C(add9)
C
Cmaj7
you.
Be brave, young lov - ers, and fol - low your
p
mf
p

C6
Cmaj7
C6
G7/B
star, be brave and faith - ful and true.
Fm/C
G7/B
E♭/B♭
6fr
G7/B
Dm7
Cling ver - y close to each oth - er to - night—
I've been in
Dm7/G
G7
C
F/A
C7sus/G
3fr
love like you.
I know how it feels to have
mf
mp
F/A
C7sus/G
3fr
F/A
C7sus/G
3fr
C7
F
wings on your heels, and to fly down a street in a trance.

E7
Am
You fly down a street on a chance that you'll meet, and you
Dm7
Dm7/G
G7
meet — not real - ly by chance. Don't
p
C(add9)
C
Cmaj7
C6
Cmaj7
cry, young lov - ers, what - ev - er you do, don't cry be -
C6
G7/B
Fm/C
G7/B
cause I'm a - lone. All of my mem - 'ries are

E♭/B♭
6fr
G7/B
Dm7
G7
hap - py to - night —
I've had a love of my
C7
F/A
Fm/A♭
own,
I've had a love of my
mf
C+/G
C6/G
Dm
E♭/G
3fr
G7
own, like yours,
I've had a love of my
cresc. ed allargando
1
C6
G7
2
C6
own.
Hel -
own.
mf a tempo
p
f

A LITTLE BIT IN LOVE

from WONDERFUL TOWN

Music by LEONARD BERNSTEIN
Lyrics by BETTY COMDEN and ADOLPH GREEN

haps a lit - tle bit more.
(rhythmically)
p
When he looks at me, ev - 'ry-thing's ha - zy and all out of fo - cus.
p sub.
When he touch-es me, I'm in the spell of a strange ho - cus po - cus.
It's so I don't know. I'm so I don't know. I don't

cresc.
poco rit.
a tempo
know, but I know if it's love, then it's love - ly! Mm, It's so
cresc.
poco rit.
a tempo
nice to be a - live When you meet some - one who be -
witch - es you. Will he be my all, or did
freely
freely
I just fall a lit - tle bit, a lit - tle bit in

a tempo
love?
mf espr.
a tempo
pp
Mm.

p
When he looks at me, ev - 'ry-thing's ha - zy and all out of fo - cus.
p sub.
When he touch - es me, I'm in the spell of a strange ho - cus po - cus.
It's so I don't know. I'm so I don't know. I don't
cresc.
know, but I know if it's love, then it's love - ly!
poco rit.

p a tempo
Mm, It's so nice to be a - live When you
p a tempo
meet some - one who be - witch - es you. Will he
freely
be my all, or did I just fall a lit - tle bit, a
freely
lit - tle bit in love.
pp

BAUBLES, BANGLES AND BEADS

from KISMET

Words and Music by ROBERT WRIGHT and GEORGE FORREST
(Music Based on Themes of A. BORODIN)

Dm7/G
G7
Cmaj7
C/E
E♭dim7
span - gles, my heart will sing, sing - a - ling - a,
Dm7
Dm7/G
G7
Cmaj7
wear - ing bau - bles, ban - gles and beads.
F♯m7
B13
7fr
Emaj9
I'll glit - ter and gleam so,
Amaj7
E♭7
A♭maj7
A♭/C
3fr
E7/B
make some - bod - y dream so, that

B♭m7
B♭m7/E♭
E♭7
A♭maj7
Cm7♭5
F7♭9
some - day he may buy me a ring, ring - a - ling - a.
B♭m7
B♭m7/E♭
E♭9
A♭maj7
Cm7♭5
F7♭9
I've heard that's where it leads, wear - ing
B♭m7
B♭m7/E♭
E♭9
1
A♭
A♭/C
E7/B
bau - bles, ban - gles and beads.
2
A♭
D♭/A♭
A♭maj9
A♭maj7
beads.

HEY THERE
from THE PAJAMA GAME

Words and Music by RICHARD ADLER
and JERRY ROSS

G
E♭
Am7
D9
D7
G7
cloud, though she won't throw a crumb to you, you
C13
C7♭9
Fm7
B9
B♭9
think some-day she'll come to you; bet - ter for -
E♭
B7
Fm7
B♭7♭9
E♭
B7
Fm7
B♭9
B♭7
get her, her with her nose in the air, she has you danc - ing
C9
Fm7/B♭
B♭7
B♭m7
E♭13
E9
E♭9
on a string, break it and she won't care! Won't you

A♭maj7
Am7♭5
D7♯5
D7
Gm7
take this ad - vice I hand you like a broth - er?
C9
C7♭9
Fm7
A♭m6
Gm7
Or are you not see - ing things too clear, are you too much in love to
C7
Fm
Gm7
A♭maj7
B♭7♭9
hear, is it all go - ing on one ear and out the
1
D/E♭
E♭
Fm7
B♭7
oth - er?
2
D/E♭
E♭
E♭6/9
oth - er?
mp

HEART

from DAMN YANKEES

Words and Music by RICHARD ADLER
and JERRY ROSS

Fmaj7
F6
D7
Dm7
G7
mope,
noth - in's half as bad as it may ap - pear,
Gm7
C11 Gm7♭5
F
N.C.
Cm7
3fr
wait - 'll next year and hope.
When your luck is bat - tin' ze - ro,
F
F7♯5
B♭maj7
B♭6
N.C.
get your chin up off the floor;
mis - ter, you can be a
Dm7
G7
C7
Cdim
3fr
he - ro,
you can o - pen an - y door. There's noth - in' to it, but to

C7 D7♯5 Gm7 D♭9 C7 C7♯5
8fr
do it, you've got - ta have heart, miles 'n' miles 'n' miles of
Fmaj7 F6 D7 Dm7 G7
heart, oh, it's fine to be a ge - nius, of course, but
Gm7 C11 Cm6 D7 Gm7 C7
3fr
keep that old horse be-fore the cart, first, you've got - ta have
1 F F♯dim Gm7 D7♯5
9fr
heart! You've got - ta have
2 F B♭9 Bdim F6
heart.
8vb

TILL THERE WAS YOU

from Meredith Willson's THE MUSIC MAN

By MEREDITH WILLSON

E♭maj7
Edim7
Fm7
birds in the sky, but I nev - er saw them
A♭m6
E♭
G♭dim7
Fm7
B♭7♭9
wing - ing. No, I nev - er saw them at all till there was
E♭6
A♭maj7
E♭maj9
A♭
you. And there was mu - sic and
mf
Adim7
E♭
C7
C7♯5
there were won - der - ful ros - es, they tell me, in

Fm7
F7
B♭7
sweet fra - grant mead - ows of dawn, and
dim.
B♭7♯5
B♭7♭9
E♭maj7
Edim7
Fm7
6fr
3fr
dew. There was love all a - round, but I nev - er heard it
8va
p
A♭m6
E♭
G♭dim7
Fm7
B♭7♭9
4fr
3fr
4fr
sing - ing. No, I nev - er heard it at all till there was
3
1
E♭6
A♭maj7
E♭maj9
you. And there was
2
E♭6
A♭maj9
E♭maj13
3fr
6fr
you.
molto rit.

I'VE GROWN ACCUSTOMED TO HER FACE

from MY FAIR LADY

Words by ALAN JAY LERNER
Music by FREDERICK LOEWE

E♭
E♭maj7
E♭6
Fm7
B♭7
na - ture to me now, like breath-ing out and breath-ing in.
na - ture to me now, like breath-ing out and breath-ing in.
E♭maj7
E♭6
A♭6
D7/A
E♭/B♭
C7♯5
I was se - rene - ly in - de - pen - dent and con - tent be - fore we met;
I'm ver - y grate - ful she's a wom - an and so eas - y to for - get,
Fm7
B♭7
G7♯5
C7♯5
F9
A♭m
sure - ly I could al - ways be that way a - gain and yet, I've grown ac - cus - tomed to her looks, ac -
rath - er like a hab - it one can al - ways break and yet, I've grown ac - cus - tomed to the trace of
E♭/B♭
Gm7
Fm7
B♭9
1
E♭
2
E♭6
cus - tomed to her voice, ac - cus - tomed to her face. I've grown ac -
some - thing in the air, ac - cus - tomed to her face.
3fr
6fr
8fr
4fr

LOOK WHO'S IN LOVE

from REDHEAD

Words and Music by DOROTHY FIELDS
and ALBERT HAGUE

A♭6/E♭
B♭m7
E♭7
A♭6
3fr
Fm
Fm(maj7)
Fm7
in our arms?
No one but us!
Who is tug - ging
B♭7
B♭m7/E♭
6fr
E♭13♭9
6fr
A♭(add2)
4fr
at my heart?
Who is?
You is!
Who was sur -
F7
B♭m7
B♭m7/E♭
6fr
E♭7
D♭
prised?
We were...
Well, were-n't we?
You look as
G7
C7
Fm7
A♭7
4fr
D♭maj7
tip - sy as I.
Hear me say, "Hey

Gb9
Ab/Eb
1
Gb9
Cm/Eb
F7#5(b9)
peo - ple, How blessed can I be?" Look who's in
rit.
Bbm
Eb13b9
Ab
Bbm7
Eb13b9
2
Gb7
love with me.
be?" (Whee!)
Ab
F9#5
Bb9
Eb7
Ab
Fm7
C7
F7
Look who's in love, look who's in love,
a tempo
Bbm7
Gb9
Eb13b9
Abmaj6/9
look who's in love with me!
rit.

THE SOUND OF MUSIC

from THE SOUND OF MUSIC

Lyrics by OSCAR HAMMERSTEIN II
Music by RICHARD RODGERS

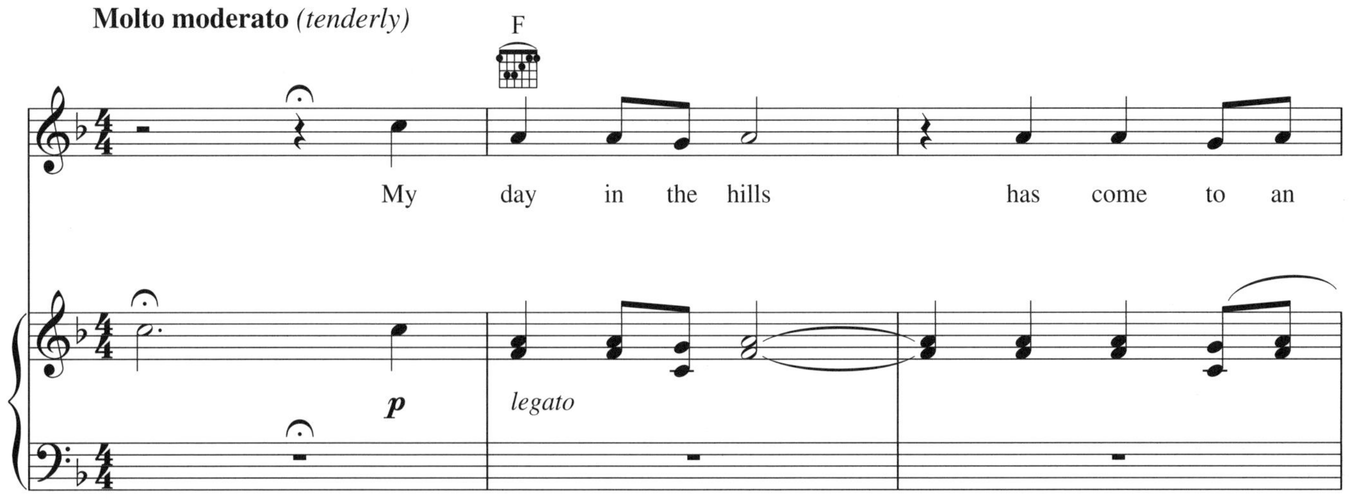

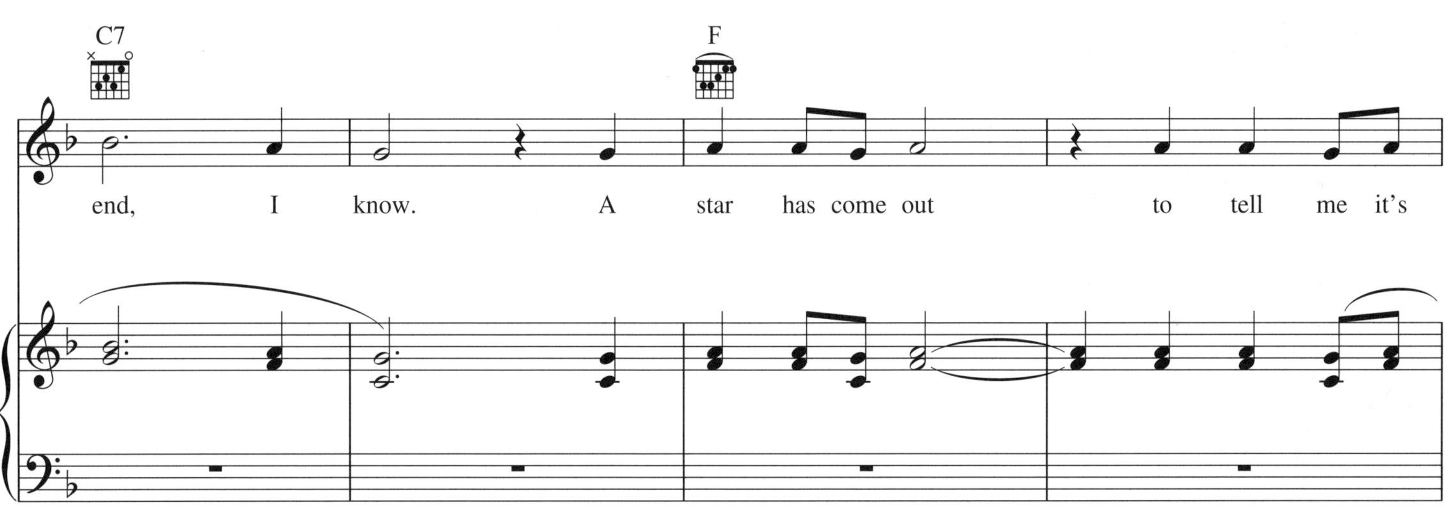

C7
F
Fm6
voic - es that urge me to stay. So I pause and I wait and I
E♭
3fr
C7
F
Gm
3fr
C7
lis - ten for one more sound, For one more love - ly thing that the hills might
rit.
Refrain (moderately, with warm expression)
F
F(add9)
E/F
say. The hills are a - live with the sound of mu - sic,
più rit.
p a tempo
F6
B♭/D
With songs they have sung for a thou - sand years.
3

C7
F(add9)
E/F
The hills fill my heart with the sound of mu - sic.
F/A
B♭/D
C6
C7
F
My heart wants to sing ev - 'ry song it hears.
B♭
B♭dim7
F/A
F/C
B♭
B♭dim7
My heart wants to beat like the wings of the birds that rise from the lake to the
mp
F/A
F/C
B♭
B♭dim7
F/A
F/C
G7/D
D♭7♭5
8fr
trees. My heart wants to sigh like a chime that flies from a church on a

C
F/A
B♭
B♭dim7
F/A
F/C
breeze, To laugh like a brook when it trips and falls o - ver
B♭
B♭dim7
F/A
F/C
Dm
Dm6
Am
stones in its way, To sing through the night like a
Dm
G7
C
C7
F(add9)
lark who is learn - ing to pray. I go to the hills
mp
E/F
when my heart is lone - ly. I

F6/9
B♭/D
know I will hear what I've heard be - fore.
B♭m/D♭
F/C
Am/C
My heart will be blessed with the sound of
mf più espressivo
B♭
Gm7
Am/C
C7
mu - sic And I'll sing once
dim.
1
F
Fdim
8fr
Gm7/F
C7
2
F
more. The more.
p
mp

WHEN DID I FALL IN LOVE

from the Musical FIORELLO!

Words by SHELDON HARNICK
Music by JERRY BOCK

Out of the house ten sec-onds and I miss him, I miss him more
with each good - bye. Out of the house ten sec - onds and I miss him,
and no one's more as - ton-ished than I. I nev - er
Rubato
once pre - tend-ed that I loved him; when did I start this change of
pp
p
p
(mp)
(pp)

Slowly and tenderly
heart?
When did I fall in love?
What night?
Which day?
When did I first be - gin to feel this way?
How could the
mo - ment pass, un - felt, ig - nored?
Where was the blind - ing flash?
Where was the crash - ing chord?
When did I fall in love?
I can't
pp
(pp)
p
f

re - call,
not that it mat - ters at all.
pp
pp
cresc.
f
rit.
It does - n't mat - ter when or why or how, as long as
L.H.
L.H.
L.H.
L.H.
rit.
ten.
I love him now.
When did re - spect first be - come af - fec - tion? When did af - fec - tion

sud-den-ly soar?
What a strange and beau-ti-ful touch
that I love him so much,
when I did-n't be-fore.
When did I fall in love?
Which night?
Which day?
When did I first be-gin to feel this way?
How could the mo-ment pass, un-felt,
(p)
p
pp
mf
cresc.

ig - nored?
Where was the blind - ing flash?
Where was the crash - ing chord?
cresc.
f
When did I fall in love?
I can't re - call,
not that it
p
pp
mat - ters at all.
I'm where I want to be,
his love,
p
cresc.
f
L.H.
L.H.
L.H.
rit.
ten.
his wife
un - til the end of my life.
(L.H.)
L.H.
rit.
ff

PUT ON A HAPPY FACE

from BYE BYE BIRDIE

Lyric by LEE ADAMS
Music by CHARLES STROUSE

G7 C7 F7 B♭7 E♭maj7 E♭7 E♭6
mask of trag - e - dy, it's not your style;
A♭maj7 D7 G7 C7 F7 Fm7
You'll look so good that you'll be glad ya' de - cid - ed to smile!
B♭9 E♭ E♭6 Gm7 C7
Pick out a pleas - ant out - look,
Fm7 B♭9 Fm7 B♭9 E♭ E♭6
stick out that no - ble chin; Wipe off that "full of
3fr

Gm7
C7
Fm7
B♭9
B♭m7
E♭7
doubt" look,
slap on a hap - py
grin! And
A♭maj7
B♭9
E♭
Fm7
B♭7
spread
sun - shine all
o - ver the
G7♯5
G7
C9
F9
Fm7
B♭9
place, just
put on a
hap - py
1
E♭
E♭6
Fm7
B♭7
face!
2
E♭
E♭6
Fm7
E♭
face!

COMEDY TONIGHT

from A FUNNY THING HAPPENED ON THE WAY TO THE FORUM

Words and Music by
STEPHEN SONDHEIM

G
C
F
D7
Some - thing for ev - 'ry - one, a com - e - dy to - night!
Some - thing for ev - 'ry - one, a com - e - dy to - night!
G
C
D
B
Noth - ing with kings, noth - ing with crowns.
Noth - ing of Gods, noth - ing of Fate.
F
G
Am
B
C
D11
5fr
Bring on the lov - ers, li - ars and clowns!
Weigh - ty af - fairs will just have to wait.
G
C
D
G
C
D
Old sit - u - a - tions, new com - pli - ca - tions,
Noth - ing that's for - mal, noth - ing that's nor - mal,

G
Am
G
B♭m7
Noth - ing por - ten - tous or po - lite;
No re - ci - ta - tions to re - cite!
Am7
1
D7
G
Trag - e - dy to - mor - row, com - e - dy to - night!
O - pen up the cur - tain,
Am
D
G
Am
D
2
com - e - dy
D7
G
Am
D
G
to - night!
ff
sfz

I BELIEVE IN YOU

from HOW TO SUCCEED IN BUSINESS WITHOUT REALLY TRYING

By FRANK LOESSER

Am7 D9 C C♯m7 F♯
up - turned chin and the grin of im - pet - u - ous
bold brave spring of the ti - ger that quick-ens your
B C B Cmaj7 D♭7 D7
youth.
walk.
Oh, I be - lieve in
G D G Cmaj7 D♭7 D7 Gsus G D
you, I be - lieve in you.
1 G G♯dim7
I hear the
2 G E♭7 A♭ B♭m7 E♭7♭5
And when my faith in my

A♭
B♭m7
D♭9
fel - low man
all but falls
a -
Cm7
F7
B♭
Cm7
F7
part,
I've but to feel your hand
B♭
Gm7
C7
D7sus
D7
grasp - ing mine
and I take heart,
I take heart.
rit.
G♯dim
Am7
D9
C
C♯m7
F♯7
To see the cool
clear
eyes of a seek - er of wis - dom and

Bm
C
Bm
G♯dim7
Am7
truth,
yet there's that slam
D9
C
C♯m7
F♯
B
C
bang
tang
rem - i - nis - cent of gin and ver - mouth.
B
Cmaj7
D♭7
D7
G
Oh, I be - lieve in you,
Cmaj7
D♭7
D7
Cmaj7
D11
Gmaj7
I be - lieve in you.

HELLO, DOLLY!

from HELLO, DOLLY!

Music and Lyric by
JERRY HERMAN

Cm
Cm7
F7
B♭6/D
D♭dim7
Dol - ly, you're still glow - in', you're still crow - in', you're still go - in'
F7
B♭
Gm
strong. We feel the room sway - in', for the band's
Fm7
B♭7
Fm7
B♭7
E♭maj7
E♭6
play - in' one of your old fav - 'rite songs from 'way back when.
Am7♭5/D
D7
Gm
Dm
Gm
So,
take her wrap, fel - las. Find her an emp - ty
gol - ly gee, fel - las, find her a va - cant

Dm
C9
C9♯5
1
Cm7
F9
lap, fel - las.
knee, fel - las.
Dol - ly - 'll nev - er go a - way a -
B♭
Bdim7
Cm7
F7
2
Cm7
F9
gain!
Hel - go a - way,
C13
C9♯5
Cm7
F9
C9
C9♯5
Dol - ly - 'll nev - er go a - way, Dol - ly - 'll nev - er
Cm7
F9
B♭
F7
B♭
go a - way a - gain!

APPLAUSE

from the Broadway Musical APPLAUSE

Lyric by LEE ADAMS
Music by CHARLES STROUSE

Dm
Dm/C
B♭
Gm7♭5
You're think - ing you're through,
You're catch - ing the flu,
that no - bod - y cares,
your bank ac - count's bare.
Dm
G7
Gm7/C
C7
Gm7/C
C7
then sud - den - ly, you
You're lone - ly and blue,
hear it start - ing!
then you hear it!
F
F(no5th)
And some - how you're in charge a - gain,
And all at once you know a - gain,
and it's a ball.
what life is for.
F6
Fmaj7
Trum - pets all sing,
Cares dis - ap - pear
life seems to swing,
soon as you hear

Dm
Dm7
B♭
C7
Dm
Dm7/C
Gm/B♭
and you're the king of it all, 'cause,
that hap-py au-di-ence roar, 'cause
you've had a taste of
F/C
B♭m6/D♭
2fr
Fmaj9
F6
Gm7/C
C7
the sound that says love,
ap-plause, ap-plause, ap-
1
F
Dm7
Gm7
C7
2
F
plause!
plause!
Repeat and Fade

SUNRISE, SUNSET

from the Musical FIDDLER ON THE ROOF

Words by SHELDON HARNICK
Music by JERRY BOCK

Moderately slow Waltz tempo

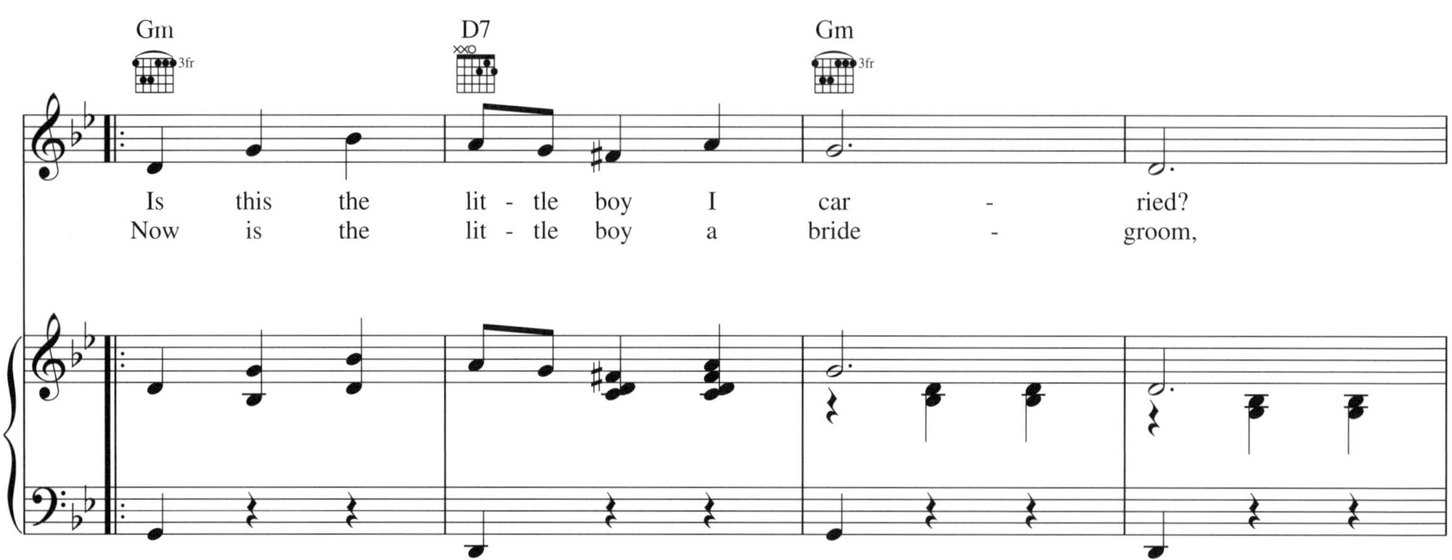

G7 Cm A A7
mem-ber grow - ing old - er, when did
can - o - py I see them, side by
D7#5 Gm D7 Gm
they? When did she get to be a beau -
side. Place the gold ring a-round her fin -
D7 Gm G7
ty? When did he grow to be so tall?
ger. Share the sweet wine and break the glass.
Cm G7 Cm A7
Was - n't it yes - ter - day when they were
Soon the full cir - cle will have come to

D
D7
D+
D7
small?
pass.
Gm
D7
Gm
D7
Gm
3fr
Sun - rise, sun - set, sun - rise, sun - set, swift - ly
G7
Cm
flow the days. Seed - lings turn
F7
B♭maj7
B♭6
Am7
D7
o - ver-night to sun - flow'rs, blos - som - ing e - ven as we

Gm
D7
Gm
gaze.
Sun - rise,
sun - set,
sun - rise,
D7
Gm
G7
sun - set,
swift - ly
fly the years;
Cm
F7
B♭maj7
B♭6
Am7
one sea - son
fol - low - ing
an - oth - er,
la - den with
D7
1
Gm
2
Gm
hap - pi - ness and
tears.
tears.
rit.

THE IMPOSSIBLE DREAM
(The Quest)
from MAN OF LA MANCHA

Lyric by JOE DARION
Music by MITCH LEIGH

1
Cm
3fr
F7
run where the brave dare not go, to
2
Cm
3fr
Cm7
3fr
F7
Cm7/F
8fr
reach the un - reach - a - ble star! This is my
B♭
Gm7
quest, to fol - low that star, no mat - ter how
Dm
B♭/D
E♭6
hope - less, no mat - ter how far; to fight for the

Gm
3fr
G♭
G♭+
right with - out ques - tion or pause, to be will - ing to
B♭/F
G♭+
Gm
3fr
A♭
4fr
Cm
3fr
marchin - to hell for a heav - en - ly cause! And I know, if I'll on - ly be
f
ff
A♭
4fr
D
true to this glo - ri - ous quest, that my
E♭6
A7
heart will lie peace - ful and calm, when I'm laid to my

E♭m
F7
B♭(add2)
B♭
B♭(add2)
B♭
rest. And the world will be bet-ter for this, that one
E♭maj7
E♭maj7
E♭6
man, scorned and cov - ered with scars, still
Dm
Dm7
Cm7
strove with his last ounce of cour - age, to
B♭/F
Cm7/F
B♭
reach the un-reach-a - ble stars.
rall.
a tempo

CABARET

from the Musical CABARET

Words by FRED EBB
Music by JOHN KANDER

F♯dim7
Em/G
A9
5fr
cab - a - ret, old chum,
Dm7
G9
9fr
1
C
Dm7
G9
9fr
come to the cab - a - ret.
2
C
Fm
ret. Come taste the wine, come hear the
C
Am
Am(maj7)
Am7
D9
4fr
band, come blow the horn, start cel - e - brat - ing,

G7
C(add9)
G9
9fr
G9♯5
3fr
right this way, your ta - ble's wait - ing.
No use per - mit - ting some
Start by ad - mit - ting from
C(add9)
G7♯5
C
Cmaj9
proph - et of doom
to wipe ev - 'ry smile a -
cra - dle to tomb
is - n't that long a
Gm7
C7
F
F♯dim7
To Coda
way;
stay;
Life is a cab - a -
Em7/G
A9
5fr
Dm7
F/G
C
ret, old chum,
come to the cab - a - ret.

D.S. al Coda
CODA
Em7/G
A9
5fr
Come taste the
ret, old chum,
F
F♯dim7
on - ly a cab - a -
Em7/G
A9
5fr
Dm7
ret, old chum, so come to the
F/G
C
G9♯5
3fr
C
cab - a - ret.
sfz

HALLELUJAH, BABY

from HALLELUJAH, BABY!

Words by BETTY COMDEN and ADOLPH GREEN
Music by JULE STYNE

F G A
Glo - ry be, had a vi - sion, big de - ci - sion!
Gm7 C Gm7
I be - lieve, I be - lieve in me.
C Gm7 C F B♭ F7 F F7
No doubt I
F B♭ F7 F F7 F
used to doubt like Mo - ses in the dark when all the

B♭
F7
F
F7
B♭
lights went out! Hal - le - lu - jah, ba - by!
F
G
A
Glo - ry be, light the ne - on, turn - ing me on!
Gm7
A♭
B♭9
C
C7
I be - lieve, I be - lieve in me.
ff
F9♯5
B♭6/9
Fmaj7
F6
F
F7
Yes - ter - day, hal - le - lu, a

B♭m
G♭
C7sus
C7
F
B♭
F7
F
F7
lost,
lost
lamb,
but
F9♯5
7fr
B♭6/9
B♭9♯5
A7sus
A7
Fm6
Dm
now,
to
-
day!
Hal - le - lu,
B♭m6
6fr
F
D♭9
A♭m7
4fr
wham!
I
know
who
I
am!
C9♯5
C7
F
B♭
F7
F
F7
Yes,
I,
I

F
B♭
F7
got the call,
I'll hire a hall, tell
one and all that life's a ball.
Hal - le - lu - jah,
ba - by!
Look at me,
yeah! This pig - eon
G
A
got re - li - gion!
1
Gm7
C7
I be - lieve,
I be - lieve in

2
F
B♭
F7
C
C7
Gm7
C7♭5
7fr
Fmaj7
Am7
C7♯9
G♭9♭5
8fr
F6/9
me.
Hal - le - lu, hal - le - lu - jah! Hal - le - lu, hal - le - lu, hal - le - lu - jah, hal - le - lu - jah, glo - ry be,
I be - lieve in
me!

MAMA, LOOK SHARP

from 1776

Words and Music by
SHERMAN EDWARDS

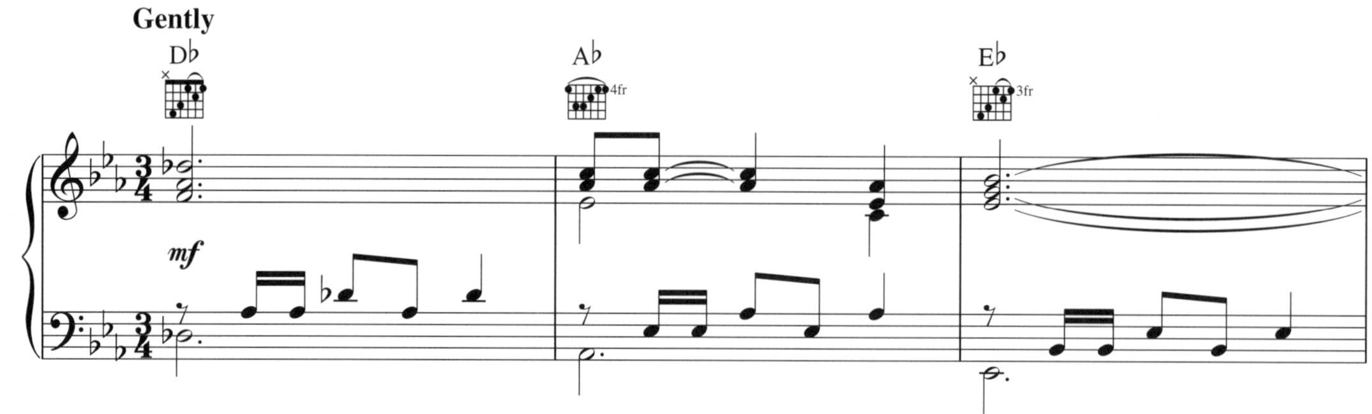

E♭
G♭
A♭
E♭
Ma - ma, hey, Ma - ma, look sharp! Here I
B♭
F
D♭
A♭
be. Hey! Hey! Ma - ma, look
E♭
G♭
A♭
sharp! My eyes are wide o - pen, my
E♭
A♭
E♭
G♭
face to the sky, is that you I'm hear - in' in the

E♭
A♭
B♭
E♭
G♭
A♭
3fr
4fr
tall grass near - by?
Ma - ma, come find me be -
E♭
A♭
B♭
F
D♭
fore I do die.
Hey!
Hey!
A♭
E♭
MAMA:
Ma - ma, look sharp!
Bil - ly, dar - ling
Cm
E♭
Cm
E♭
Bil - ly, I've come to where you lay, and I'll hold you in the

Cm
Eb
Cm
mead - ow while them sol - diers march a - way. I'll
Eb
Gb
Eb
Ab
Bb
hold you in the mead - ow 'til the last light of day.
F
Db
Ab
Eb
Hey! Hey! Ma - ma, look sharp!
BILLY:
Gb
Ab
Eb
Them sol - diers, they fi - red, oh Ma! Did we

G♭
E♭
3fr
run! But then we turned 'round and the bat - tle be -
B♭
E♭
G♭
A♭
4fr
gun. Then I went un - der, oh Ma! Am I
B♭
F
D♭
done? Hey! Hey! Ma - ma, look
MAMA:
Cm
sharp! I'll close your eyes, my Bil - ly, those

E♭
Cm
E♭
Cm
3fr
eyes that can - not see, and I'll bur - y you, my Bil - ly, be -
E♭
Cm
E♭
neath the ma - ple tree. And nev - er a -
G♭
A♭
E♭
A♭
B♭
F
4fr
gain do you whis - per to me: Hey!
D♭
A♭
E♭
Hey! Ma - ma, look sharp!

BEING ALIVE

from COMPANY

Words and Music by
STEPHEN SONDHEIM

Am7/D
Dm7/G
G13
Dm7/G
Fmaj7/G
ware of be - ing a - live,
be - ing a -
Dm7/G
G13
Dm7/G
G13
C6/9
live.
Some-bod - y need me too
F/G
C6/9
G7♭9
much,
some - bod - y know me too
well,
C6/9
Am7
Fmaj9
some - bod - y pull me up
short, and put me through
hell, and give me sup -

Am7/D
Dm7/G
G13
Dm7/G
Fmaj7/G
port for be - ing a - live.
Make me a -
Dm7/G
G13
Dm7/G
Fmaj7/G
Dm7/G
G13
live,
make me a - live.
Dm7/G
Fmaj7/G
A♭/B♭
Make me con - fused,
mock me with
C
Cdim
A♭/B♭
praise,
let me be used,

Dm7/G
G13
Dm7/G
G7
3
vary my days,
but a-
3
Dm7/G
G13
G9
G9♯5
F/G
G13
lone
is a-lone,
cresc.
F6/G
G9
G9♯5
Dm7/G
G13
Dm7/G
G13
not a-live.
f
C6/9
F/G
C6/9
G7♭9
Some-bod-y crowd me with love,
some-bod-y force me to care,

C6/9
Am7
Fmaj9
some-bod - y make me come through, I'll al-ways be there as fright-ened as
Am7/D
Dm7/G
G13
Fmaj7/G
3fr
3
you, to help us sur - vive being a -
Dm7/G
G13
Dm7/G
G13
Dm7/G
G13
Dm7/G
G13
live, being a - live, being a -
C
B♭/C
C
B♭/C
C
B♭/C
C11
live.
sfz
sfz

SEND IN THE CLOWNS

from the Musical A LITTLE NIGHT MUSIC

Music and Lyrics by
STEPHEN SONDHEIM

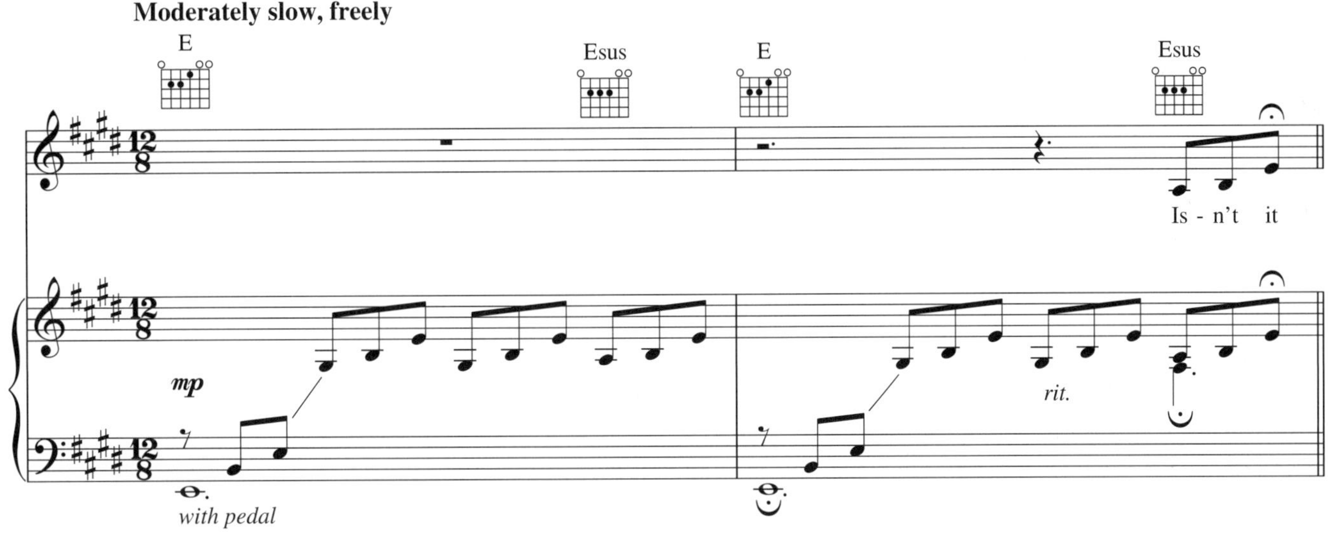

1.
B/E
A/E
Esus
2.
B/E
A/E
clowns. Is-n't it clowns? Send in the
rit.
E
G♯m
D♯m7
G♯m
D♯m7
clowns. Just when I'd stopped o-pen-ing doors, fi-nal-ly
G♯m
C♯m(add2)
C♯m
C♯m(add2)
G♯/B♯
know-ing the one that I want-ed was yours, mak-ing my
C♯m/B
C♯m/A♯
C♯m/A
G♯7sus
F♯m7♭5
en-trance a-gain with my u-su-al flair, sure of my

B6/9
B6
A/B
B/E
A/E
B/E
Esus
lines, no one is there. Is-n't it
rit.
E
Esus
E
Emaj7
rich? Is-n't it queer, los-ing my tim-ing this late in my ca-
Amaj9
Amaj9♯11
4fr
Amaj9
B13/E
A/E
F♯m/E
G♯m/E
A/E
reer? And where are the clowns? Quick, send in the clowns. Don't both-er, they're
rit.
E
Esus
E
E(add2)
here.
a tempo
rit.

WHO IS SILVIA?

from TWO GENTLEMEN OF VERONA

Words by WILLIAM SHAKESPEARE
Music by GALT MacDERMOTT

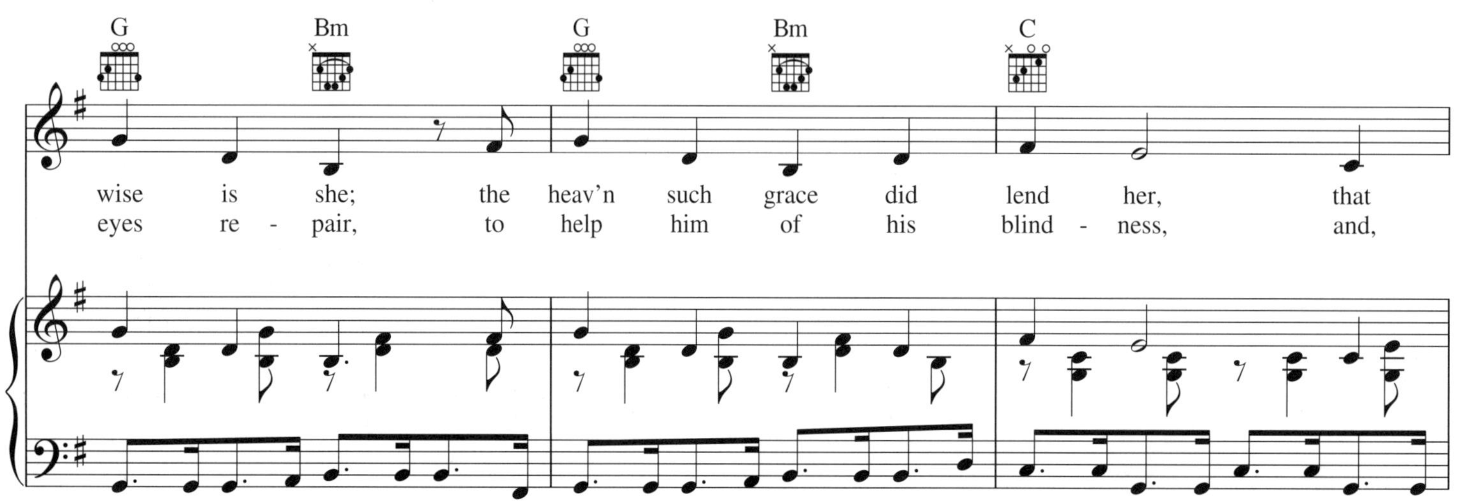

Am6
B7
Em
she might ad - mired be. Is
be - ing helped, in - hab - its there. Then to Sil - via let
F♯7
B7
Em
A7
D7
us sing, that Sil - via is ex - cel - ling;
G
Bm
G
Bm
G
Bm
she ex - cels each mor - tal thing up - on the dull earth
C
Am6
B7
Em
dwell - ing: to her let us gar - lands bring.
rit.
pp

MEASURE THE VALLEYS

from RAISIN

Words and Music by JUDD WOLDIN
and ROBERT BRITTAN

Am
Am/G
F♯dim7
F♯7♭9
3fr
wind's get - ting slow, look at where it's had to go, meas-ure the
F♯7♭9/B
B7♯9
Em
val - leys, meas - ure the hills.
A
Em
A
When a
Em
A
Em
stream's near - ly dry as bone,

A
Em
A
bet - ter count ev - 'ry turn, ev - 'ry
Em
Am
stone. When it's all run - ning
Am/G
F♯dim7
F♯7♭9
3fr
F♯7♭9/B
thin, take a look at where it's been, meas - ure the val - leys,
B7♯9
Em
A
meas - ure the hills.

Em
A
Em
When you know how a
A
Em
A
dream can fade, how a
Em
A
Em
man comes to be so a - fraid.
Am
Am/G
When you know where he's been, take a

F♯7♯9
F♯7♭9
F♯7♭9/B
B7♯9
3fr
3fr
look at him a - gain, meas-ure the val - leys, meas-ure the
poco rit.
a tempo
1
Em
A
Em
A
hills. When a
2
Em
A
F♯7♭9/B
B7♯9
hills. Meas-ure the val - leys, meas - ure the
Em
A
Em
Em6/9
hills.

THE JOINT IS JUMPIN'
from AIN'T MISBEHAVIN'

Words by ANDY RAZAF and J.C. JOHNSON
Music by THOMAS "FATS" WALLER

D A7 D A7 D A7
say that things are jump - in' leaves not a sin - gle doubt
D B♭m F C7 F F♯dim Gm7 C7
that ev - 'ry - thing is in full swing when you hear some - bod - y
F7 B♭ Bdim Cm7 F7 B♭ Bdim
shout: Here 'tis! This joint is jump - in', it's real - ly jump-
Cm7 F7 B♭ B♭7 E♭ Edim
- in'.
Come in cats an' check your hats, I mean
Ev - 'ry Mose is on his toes, I mean

B♭
F7
B♭
D
A7
this joint is jump - in'.
The pi - a - no's thump -
the joint is jump - in'.
No time for talk -
D
A7
D
A7
D
C7
F
C7
- in', the danc - ers bump - in'.
This here spot is
- in', it's time for walk - in'. (Yes!)
Grab a jug and
F
F♯dim
9fr
C7
F7
more than hot, in fact the joint is jump - in'.
cut the rug, I mean this joint is jump - in'.
B♭7
Edim
3fr
B♭7
E♭
3fr
B♭7
E♭
3fr
Check your weap - ons at the door, be sure to pay your quar - ter.
Get your pig feet, beer and gin, there's plen - ty in the kitch - en.

C7
F9
C7♯5
8fr
Burn your leath - er on the floor, grab an - y - bod - y's daugh -
Who is that that just came in? Just look at the way he's switch -
F7
B♭
Bdim
Cm7
3fr
F7
- ter. The roof is rock - in',
- in'. Don't mind the hour,
B♭
Bdim
Cm7
3fr
F7
B♭
B♭7
the neigh-bor's knock - in'. We're all bums when the
'cause I'm in pow - er. I got bail if we
E♭
3fr
Edim
3fr
1
B♭
F7
B♭
F7
wag - on comes. I mean this joint is jump - in'. Let it beat!
go to jail. I mean

2
B♭ E♭ B♭ F+ B♭ Bdim Cm7 F9
this joint is jump - in'. This joint is jump - in',
B♭ Bdim Cm7 F7 B♭ B♭7
it's real - ly jump - in'. We're all bums when the
E♭ Edim B♭ E♭ B♭ F+
wag - on comes, I mean this joint is jump - in'.
B♭ B♭7 E♭ E♭m B♭ B♭+ Gm7 C7 F7 B♭
Don't give your right name. No, no, no!

BELIEVE IN YOURSELF
(If You Believe)
from THE WIZ

Words and Music by
CHARLIE SMALLS

Gm7/C
F
feel and know you're right, be - cause
Gm7/C
the time will come a - round when you'll say it's
F
Eb/F
F7
Bbmaj7
yours. Be - lieve there's a rea - son to
lieve that you can go
mf
A7b9
5fr
Dm
Cm7
3fr
F7
be, be - lieve you can make time stand still; and
home, be - lieve you can float on air; then

B♭maj7
A7♭9
5fr
Dm
know from the mo - ment you try, if you be - lieve,
click your heels three times, if you be - lieve,
Dm♯7
Dm7/G
G7
F/C
I know you will. Be - lieve in your - self
then you'll be there. Be - lieve in your - self
Gm7/C
F/C
Gm7/C
right from the start; you'll have brains, you'll have a heart.
right from the start, be - lieve in the mag - ic right there in your heart. Be -
F/C
B♭m7
G/A
3fr
A7
Dm
You'll have cour - age to last your whole life through.
lieve all these things not be - cause I told you to,

G7
F/C
F+/B
if you be - lieve in your - self,
but be - lieve in your - self,
if you be -
Bbmaj7
F/A
Dm7
F/G
G7
lieve in your - self,
if you be - lieve in your - self as
just be - lieve in your - self as
Gm7/C
To Coda
F
Cm7
F7
D.S. al Coda
I be - lieve in you.
Be -
I be - lieve in
CODA
Dbmaj7
Gbmaj7
F
you.
rall.

WHAT I DID FOR LOVE

from A CHORUS LINE

Music by MARVIN HAMLISCH
Lyric by EDWARD KLEBAN

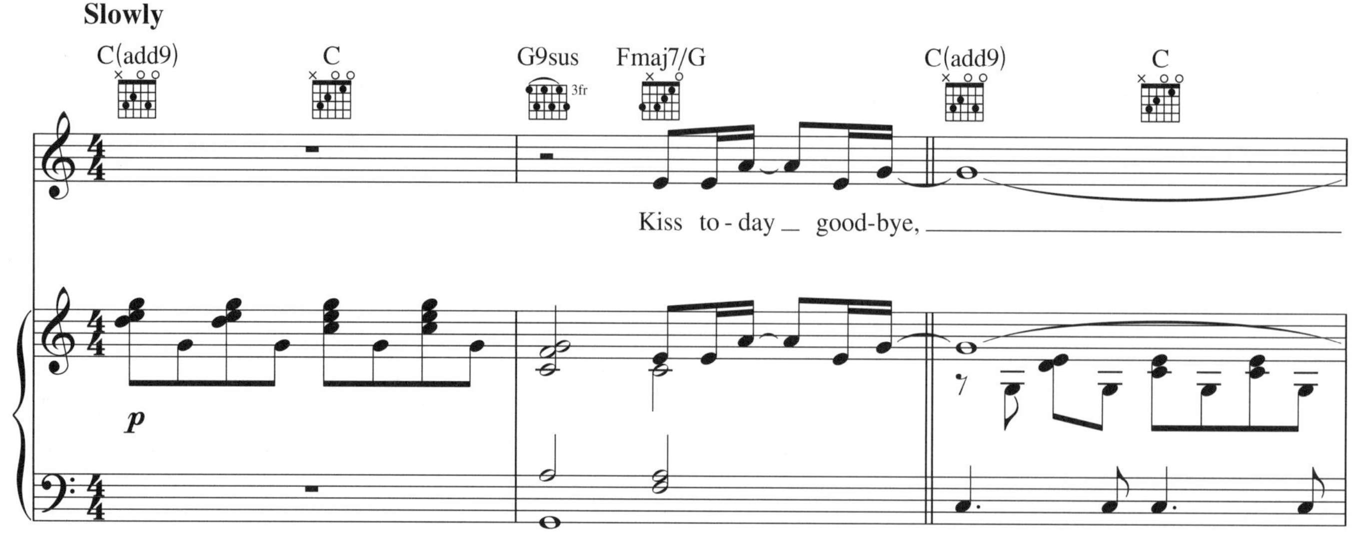

Fm
Dm7♭5
G
G/F
what I did for love,
what I did for love.
G
N.C.
C(add9)
C
A7sus
A7
Look, my eyes are dry.
The gift was ours to
Dm7
Fm
C
G/B
bor - row.
It's as if we al - ways
D9
4fr
N.C.
Fm
knew.
And I won't for - get
what I did for love,

Dm7♭5 G G/F Em7 G/D Am Am/G
what I did for love. Gone,
Fmaj7 E7sus E7 Am Am/G F♯m7♭5 B7sus B7
4fr
2fr
love is nev - er gone. As we trav - el
E(add2) E G/A A7 Dm7♭5 G7sus/D
3fr
on, love's what we'll re - mem - ber.
G7 N.C. C(add9) C A7sus A7
Kiss to - day good-bye, and point me t'ward to -

Dm7
Fm
C
G/B
mor - row.
We did what we had to
Am
Am/G
D7/F♯
Am7/E
D7
F
C/E
do.
Won't for - get, can't re - gret what I did
Dm7
G7sus
G7
C
C/B♭
Fm/A♭
N.C.
for
love...
what I did for
C
C/B♭
Fm/A♭
N.C.
C
love
what I did for
love.
rall.

TOMORROW

from the Musical Production ANNIE

Lyric by MARTIN CHARNIN
Music by CHARLES STROUSE

B♭maj7
Am7
Dm
Dm/C
clears a - way the cob - webs and the sor - row till there's
B♭maj7
C
Fm
A♭/E♭
none. When I'm stuck with a day that's gray and
D♭
E♭
3fr
A♭
4fr
A♭maj7
lone - ly, I just stick out my chin and grin and
C7sus
C7
say: Oh! the
f
mp

F
Fmaj7
B♭maj7
Am7
sun - 'll come out to - mor - row,
So you
Oh! I
got to hang on till to -
Dm
Dm/C
G♭maj7
C7sus
C7
mor - row come what may!
To -
1 (small notes are optional harmony)
F7
B♭
B♭m6
6fr
mor - row, to - mor - row, I love ya to - mor - row, you're
al - ways
on - ly
a day a - way!
The
B♭maj7/F
Gm7(add4)

2
F
Fmaj7
F7
B♭
B♭m6
6fr
mor - row, to - mor - row, I love ya to - mor - row, you're
F
C7sus
C7
F
C7sus
F
Fmaj7
al - ways
on - ly
a day a - way! To - mor - row, to - mor - row, I
F7
B♭
B♭m6
6fr
F
C7sus
C7
love ya to - mor - row, you're
al - ways
on - ly
a day a -
F
Fmaj7
B♭maj7/F
Gm7(add4)
F
way!

NOT WHILE I'M AROUND

from SWEENEY TODD, THE DEMON BARBER OF FLEET STREET

Music and Lyrics by
STEPHEN SONDHEIM

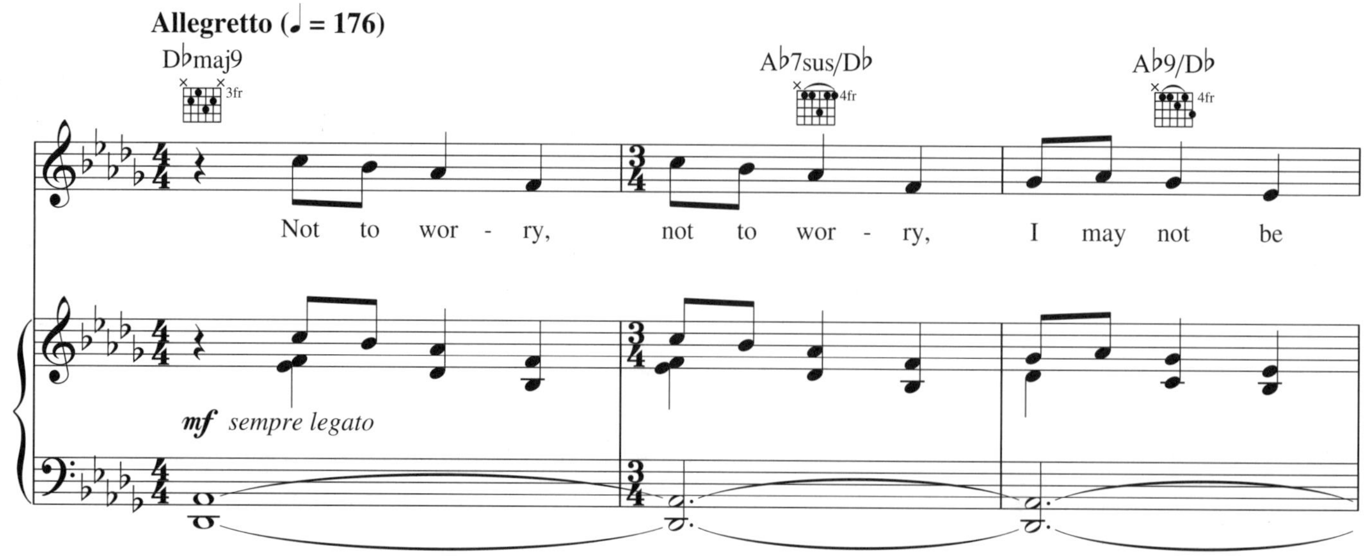

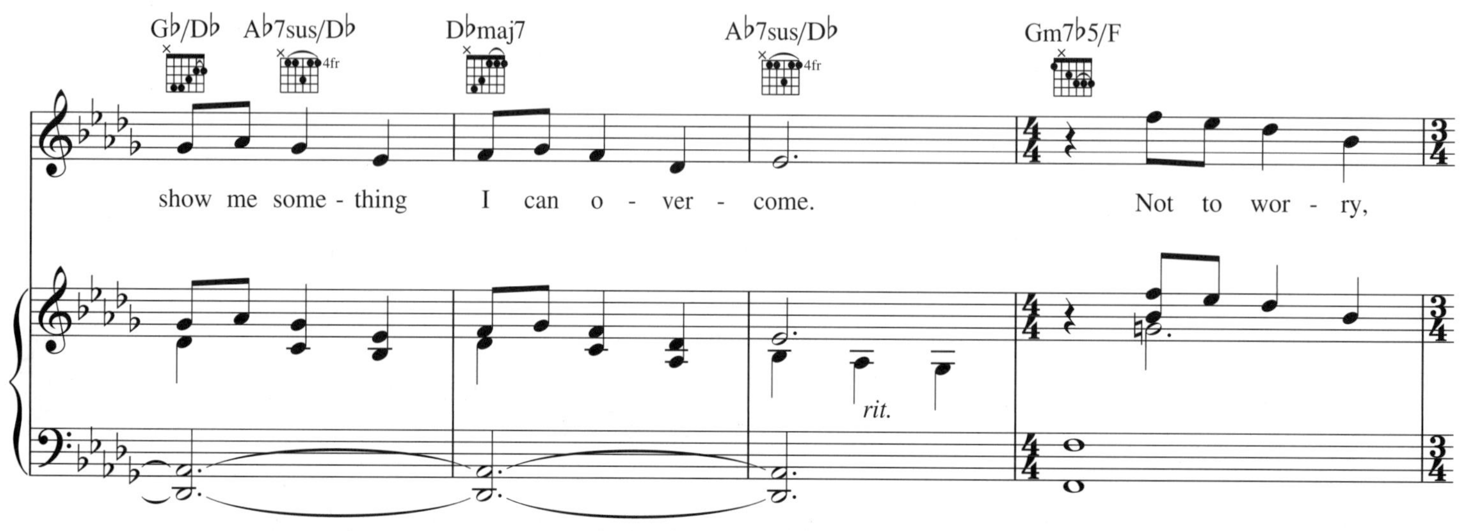

Andante placido (𝅗𝅥 = 112)
B♭sus
B♭
E♭(add9)
6fr
Poco rubato
chum.
Noth-ing's gon - na
p
R.H.
p
L.H.
harm you, not while I'm a - round.
mf
Noth-ing's gon - na harm you, no sir, not while I'm a - round.
mf
dim.
A♭maj7
B♭7/A♭
Gm9
3fr
De - mons are prowl - ing ev - 'ry - where, now - a - days.
mf poco con moto
a tempo dim.

B♭7/C
C9
F9sus
F13
A♭/C
B♭13sus
I'll send 'em howl - ing, I don't care, I got ways.
mp
dim.
B♭9
A♭/B♭
E♭6
No one's gon - na
8va
p accel.
rit.
p
a tempo
B♭/D
A♭(add9)/C
A♭m/C♭
hurt you, no one's gon - na dare.
E♭/B♭
B♭13
B♭m7
C♭
Oth - ers can de - sert you, not to wor - ry, whis - tle, I'll be there.
cresc.
mf

A♭maj7
B♭7/A♭
Gm7
De - mons-'ll charm you with a smile for a while,
f
B♭/C
A♭m/C♭
4fr
1
B♭6
A♭/B♭
4fr
but in time noth - ing can harm you, not while I'm a -
rit. e dim.
mp
E♭(add9)
6fr
2
E♭maj7/B♭
3fr
round.
noth - ing's gon - na harm you,
p a tempo
B♭9sus
4fr
E♭(add9)
6fr
not while I'm a - round.
rit.
p sub.
a tempo
rit.

DON'T CRY FOR ME ARGENTINA

from EVITA

Words by TIM RICE
Music by ANDREW LLOYD WEBBER

D♭
G♭/D♭
EVA:
It won't be eas - y, you'll think it strange when I
mf
A♭7/D♭
4fr
try to ex - plain how I feel, that I still need your love af - ter
D♭
B♭m/D♭
all that I've done. You won't be - lieve me.
E♭
3fr
E♭/D♭
All you will see is a girl you once knew, al - though she's dressed up to the

A♭/C
3fr
E♭
3fr
A♭
4fr
nines, at six - es and sev - ens with you.
poco rall.
D♭
G♭/D♭
I had to let it hap-pen, I had to change, could-n't spend all my life down at
p a tempo
A♭7/D♭
4fr
D♭
heel, look-ing out of the win-dow, stay-ing out of the sun. So I chose
B♭m/D♭
E♭
3fr
E♭/D♭
free - dom, run-ning a-round try-ing ev - 'ry-thing new, but noth-ing im-pressed me at all,

A♭/C
3fr
E♭
3fr
A♭
4fr
I never expected it to.
D♭
B♭m/D♭
D♭
Don't cry for me Argentina, the truth is I never
p
A♭
4fr
B♭m
left you. All through my wild days, my mad existence, I kept my
D♭maj7
G♭maj7
G♭6
G♭
promise, don't keep your distance.

D♭
G♭/D♭
And as for for - tune and as for fame, I
A♭7/D♭
4fr
nev - er in - vit - ed them in, though it seemed to the world_ they were
D♭
B♭m/D♭
all I de - sired. They are il - lu - sions, they're
E♭
3fr
E♭/D♭
not the so - lu - tions they prom - ised to be, the an - swer was here all the

A♭/C
E♭
A♭
3fr
3fr
4fr
time, I love you and hope you love me.
rall.
N.C.
G♭maj7
D♭
CHOIR:
Don't cry for me Ar - gen - ti - na. Mm
colla voce
p
E♭m7
D♭
A♭
B♭m
6fr
4fr
D♭maj7
G♭
D♭
EVA:
Don't cry for me Ar - gen -

ti - na, the truth is I nev - er left you. All through my
3
3
A♭7
4fr
B♭m
D♭maj7
wild days, my mad ex - is - tence, I kept my prom - ise, don't keep your
G♭maj7
dis - tance. Have I said too much, there's noth - ing more I can think of to
rall.
colla voce
Fm7
G♭maj7
say to you. But all you have to do is
tr
tr
tr
tr
with pedal

D♭
look at me to know that ev - 'ry word is true.
ff
D♭6 D♭
A♭
4fr
B♭m
D♭maj7
G♭maj7
G♭6
G♭maj7
D♭
poco rit.
p

LULLABY OF BROADWAY

from 42ND STREET

Words by AL DUBIN
Music by HARRY WARREN

F
Gm7
C7
Gm7
C9
The rum - ble of a sub - way train, the rat - tle of the
The band be - gins to go to town, and ev - 'ry - one goes
F
Gm7
C7
tax - is. The daf - fy - dils who en - ter - tain
cra - zy. You rock - a - bye your ba - by 'round
Gm7
C9
F
G7
C
A7
at An - ge - lo's and Max - ie's. When a Broad - way ba - by
'til ev - 'ry - thing gets ha - zy. "Hush - a - bye, I'll buy you
Dm7
G7
C
says "good - night," it's ear - ly in the morn - ing.
this and that," you hear a dad - dy say - ing.

A7
Dm7
Fm6
G7
Man-hat - tan ba - bies don't sleep tight
un - til the
And ba - by goes home to her flat
to sleep all
C7
F
Gm7
dawn:
day:
Good - night,
F
C9
F
F7
B♭
B♭m6
6fr
ba - by.
Good - night,
F
C9
F
milk - man's on his way.
Sleep

Gm7
F
C9
F
F7
tight, ba - by, sleep
B♭
B♭m6
6fr
1
F
C9
F
G7
tight, let's call it a day. Hey!
2
F
C7
G♯dim7
F
D♭7
4fr
Gm7
F
Dm
let's call it a day. Lis - ten to the lull - a - by of
D♭9
C9
F6/9
old Broad - way.
sffz

UNUSUAL WAY
(In a Very Unusual Way)
from NINE

Words and Music by
MAURY YESTON

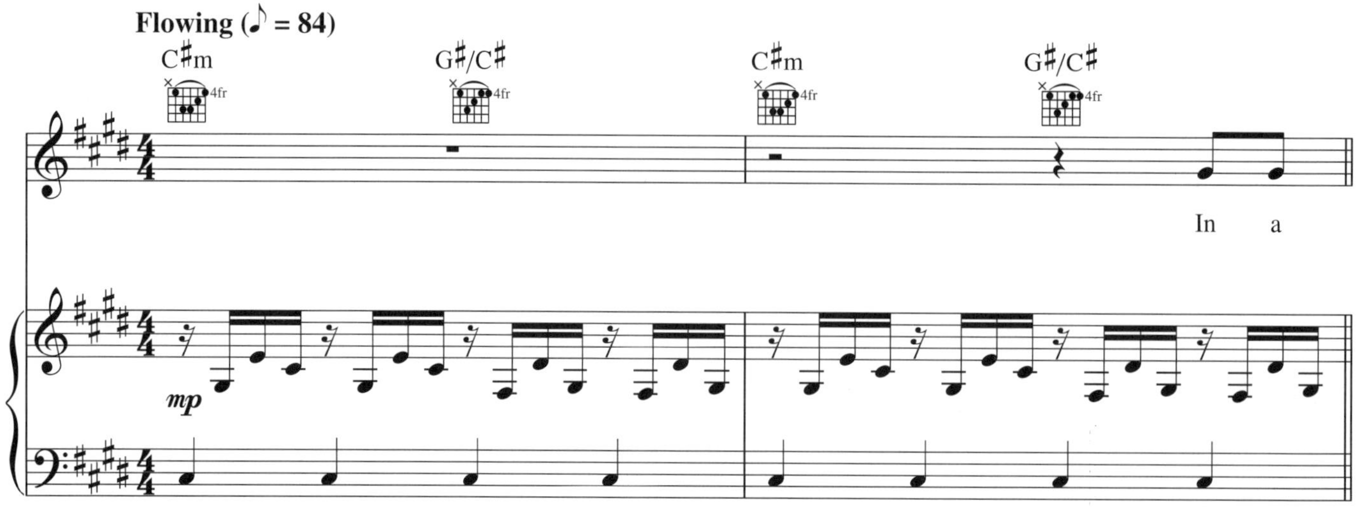

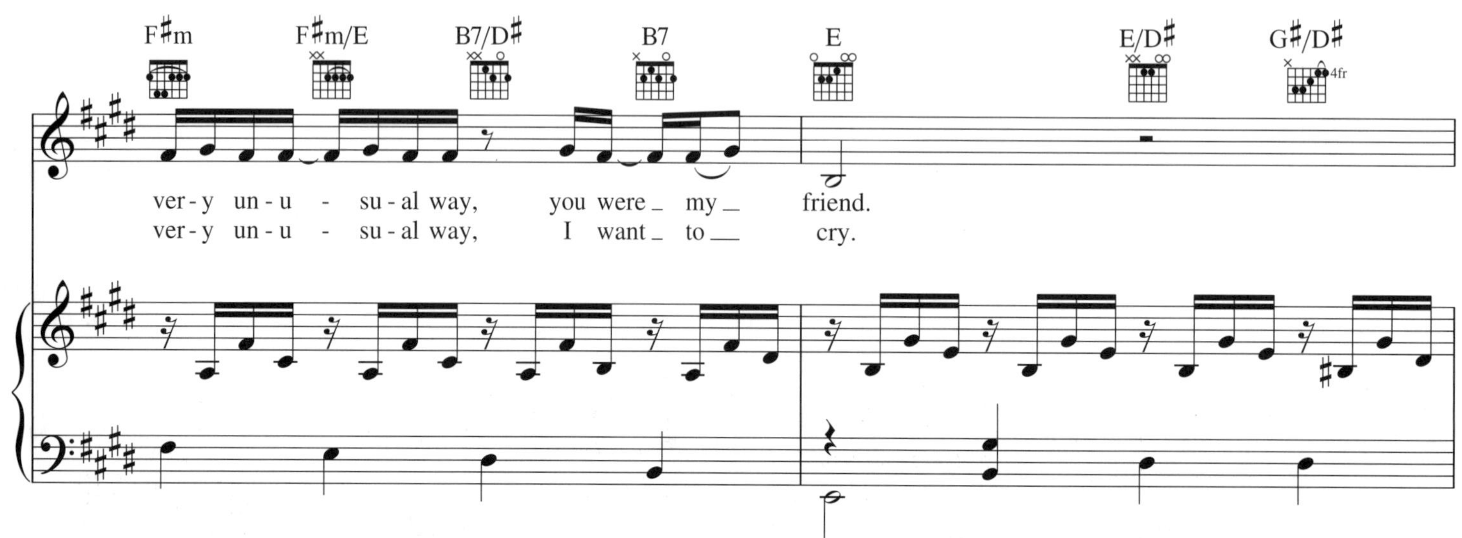

C♯m
C♯m/B
F♯/A♯
F♯m/A
G♯7
C♯m
C♯m/B
May - be it last - ed a day,
may - be it last - ed an hour,
Some-thing in - side me goes weak,
some-thing in - side me sur-ren - ders,
1
A
D
Bm7/E
Em7/A
but some-how it will nev - er end...
In a
2
A
D
Bm7/E
E7
E/D
C♯m
C♯m/B
F♯m/A
and you're the rea-son why,
you're the rea - son why.
D♯m7/G♯
4fr
6fr

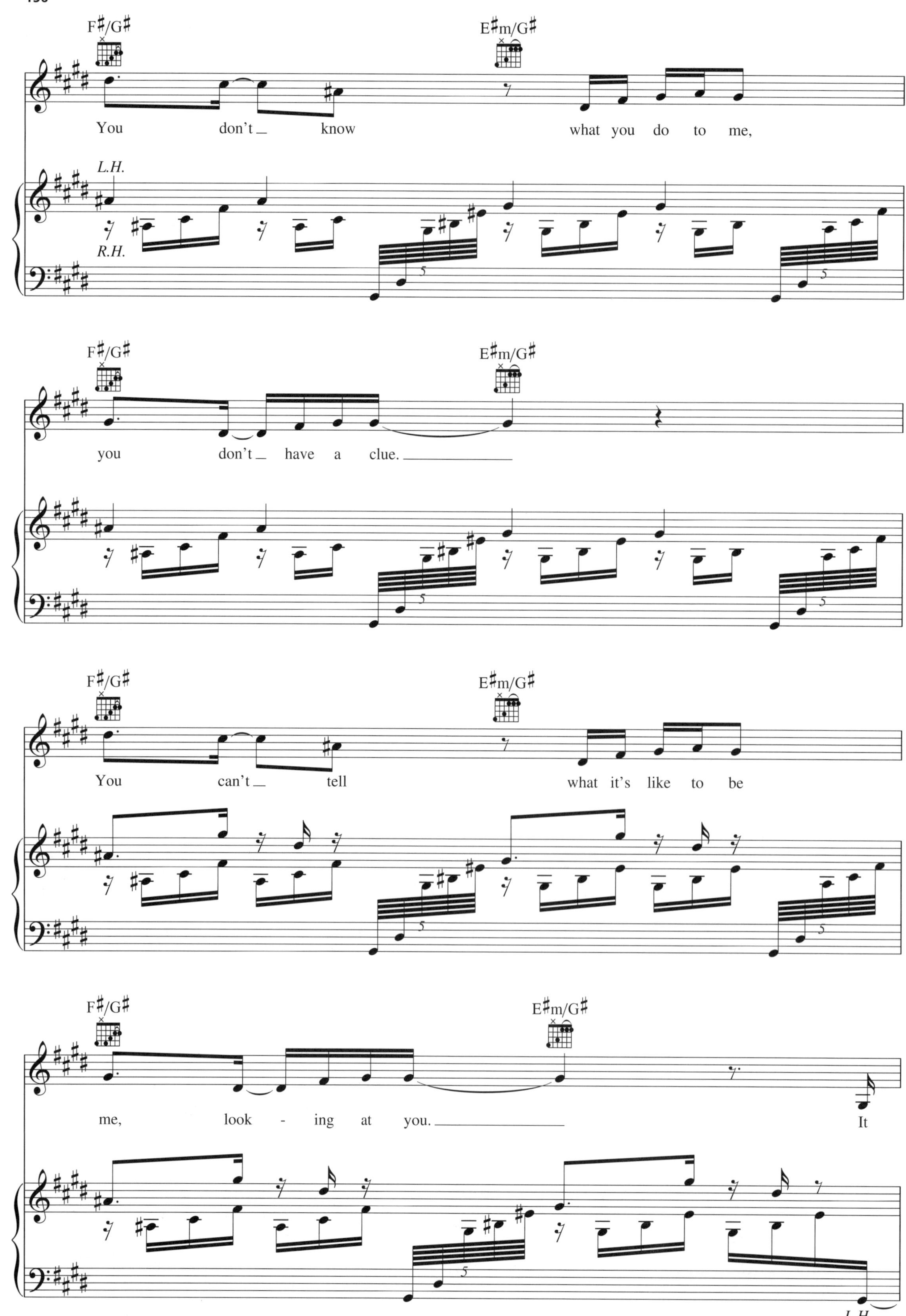
F♯/G♯
E♯m/G♯
You don't know what you do to me,
L.H.
R.H.
F♯/G♯
E♯m/G♯
you don't have a clue.
F♯/G♯
E♯m/G♯
You can't tell what it's like to be
F♯/G♯
E♯m/G♯
me, look - ing at you.
It
L.H.

F#/G#
A#m
F#
D#m7/G#
6fr
G#7
4fr
scares me so that I can hard-ly speak.
In a
C#m
4fr
G#7/D#
C#m/E
4fr
C#7/E#
F#m
F#m/G#
ver-y un-u-su-al way, I owe what I am to you.
Though at
F#m
F#m/E
B7/D#
B7
E
E/D#
G#/D#
4fr
times it ap-pears I won't stay, I nev-er go.
C#m
4fr
C#m/B
F#/A#
4fr
F#m/A
G#7
4fr
C#m
4fr
C#m/B
Spe-cial to me in my life since the first day that I met you,

A
A/C♯
D
B7/D♯
E
how could I ev - er for-get you once you had touched my soul?
G♯7/D♯
C♯m
C♯m/B
F♯/A♯
4fr
In a ver-y un-u - su-al way,
F♯m/A
A/G♯
D♯m7/G♯
6fr
you've made me
C♯
F♯/C♯
whole.
rit.

MEMORY
from CATS

Music by ANDREW LLOYD WEBBER
Text by TREVOR NUNN after T.S. ELIOT

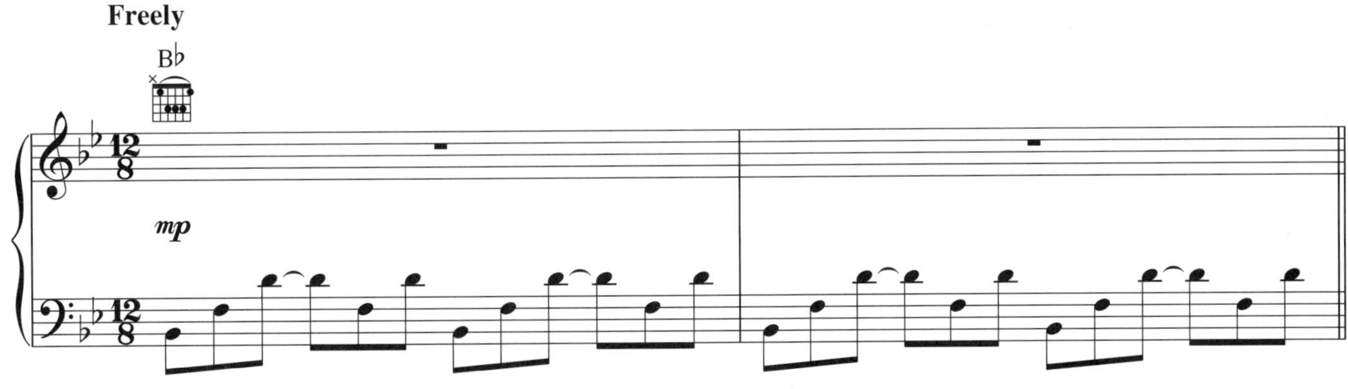

Cm
Gm
lamp - light the with-ered leaves col - lect at my feet and the
mem - ber the time I knew what hap - pi - ness was, let the
1
F
E♭/F
B♭
wind be - gins to moan.
2
F
E♭/F
B♭
mem - ory live a - gain.
Dm
Dm/E♭
Cm/E♭
Dm
Dm/E♭
Cm/E♭
Ev - 'ry street lamp seems to beat a

Dm
B♭maj7
C
F
Fmaj7
fa - tal - is - tic warn - ing.
Dm
Gm7
C7
Fmaj7
Some - one mut - ters and a street lamp gut - ters and
Dm
Dm/G
G7
C
soon it will be morn - ing.
rit.
B♭
Gm
3fr
Day - light. I must wait for the sun - rise, I must think of a
a tempo

E♭
3fr
Dm
new life and I must-n't give in. When the
Cm
3fr
Gm
3fr
dawn comes to-night will be a mem-o-ry too and a
F
E♭/F
B♭
new day will be-gin.
G♭
E♭m
6fr

C♭
B♭m
A♭m7
4fr
E♭m
6fr
D♭
C♭/D♭
4fr
G♭
B♭m
B♭m/C♭
A♭m/C♭
4fr
B♭m
B♭m/C♭
A♭m/C♭
4fr
B♭m
G♭
A♭7
4fr
Burnt out ends of smo - ky days, the stale cold smell of

D♭
B♭m7
E♭m7
6fr
morn - ing.
The street lamp dies, an - oth - er
A♭7
4fr
D♭maj7
B♭m
E♭7
night is o - ver, an - oth - er day is
A♭
4fr
A♭7
4fr
D♭
dawn - ing.
rit.
Touch me. It's so eas - y to
a tempo
B♭m
G♭
leave me all a - lone with the mem - ory of my days in the
rall.

Fm
E♭7sus
6fr
E♭m
6fr
sun. If you touch me you'll un - der - stand what
a tempo
B♭m
A♭
4fr
G♭/A♭
hap - pi - ness is. Look a new day has be -
rall.
D♭
gun.
a tempo - slightly slower

THE BEST OF TIMES

from LA CAGE AUX FOLLES

Music and Lyric by
JERRY HERMAN

Gm7♭5
C9
Fmaj7
F7
F6
F+
As for to - mor - row, well, who knows? Who knows? Who
rit.
F
C/E
Ddim
Gm7
knows? So hold this mo - ment fast
a tempo
C9
Fdim
8fr
Fmaj7
and live and love as hard as you know how.
D7♭9
4fr
Gm/E
F♯dim
9fr
Gm(maj7)
3fr
Gm7
And make this mo - ment last

Gm7♭5
C9
F
B♭/F
be - cause the best of times is now, is now, is
F
Brighter
B♭
B♭+
now.
Now,
f
B♭6
C7
Am
Am(maj7)
not some for - got - ten yes - ter - day.
Am7
Am6
Dm
Dm(maj7)
Now,

Dm7
G7
Gm
3fr
E♭/G
3fr
to - mor - row is too far a - way.
rit.
C7
F
C/E
G♯dim7
Gm(add2)
3fr
So hold this mo - ment fast,
mf
a tempo
C9
Fdim
8fr
Fmaj7
and live and love as hard as you know how.
Am7♭5
D7♭9
4fr
Gm(maj7)
3fr
Gm9
3fr
And make this mo - ment last

Gm7♭5
C9
F
B♭/F
be - cause the best of times is now, is now, is
F
Am7
E♭7
D7
G/D
D
C♯dim7
now.
The best of
molto ritard.
f
Slower
Am7
D7sus
times is now.
What's left of
D7
F♯7
F♯/G
G6
sum - mer but a fad - ed rose?

Bm7♭5
F/E
Bm7♭5/E
Am9
5fr
The best of times is now.
Am7
Am7♭5
D7
G6
As for to - mor - row, well, who knows? Who
G/D
Am/D
G/D
Am7
knows? Who knows? So hold this mo - ment fast
rit.
a tempo
D7sus
and live and love as hard as

F♯/G
G
Bm7♭5
F/E
E7♭9
you know how.
And make this
Am(maj7)
Am7
Am7♭5
D7
mo - ment last
be - cause the best of times is
G
C/G
G
Cmaj7/G
now, is now, is now, is now, is
rit. poco a poco
B♭
A♭
4fr
G6
now.

MOONFALL

from THE MYSTERY OF EDWIN DROOD

Words and Music by
RUPERT HOLMES

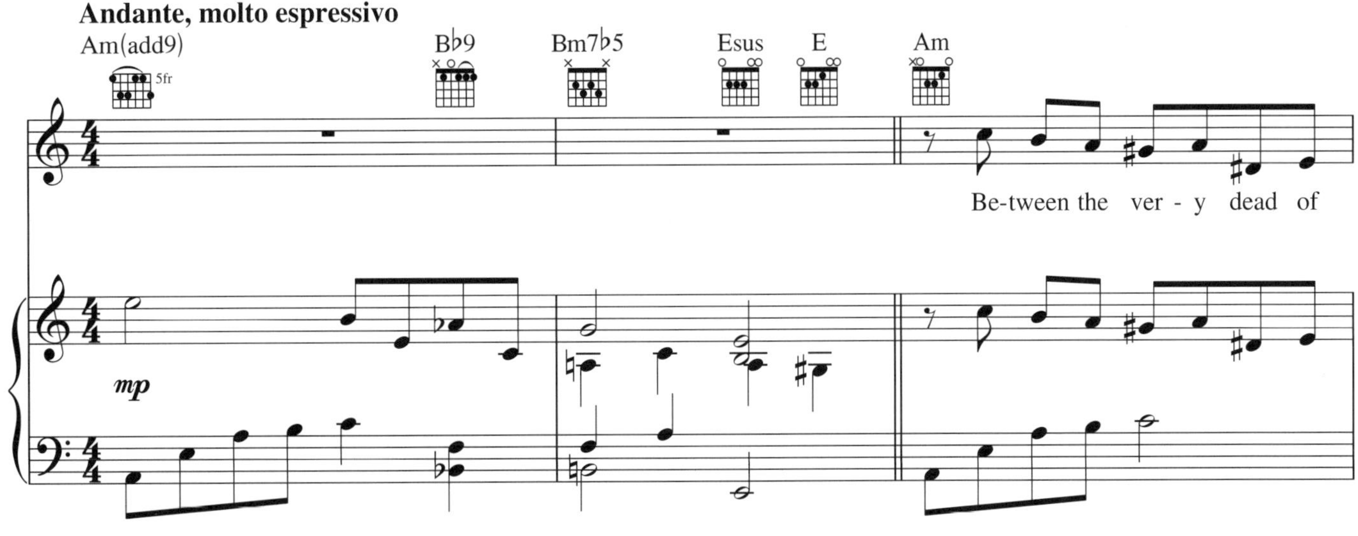

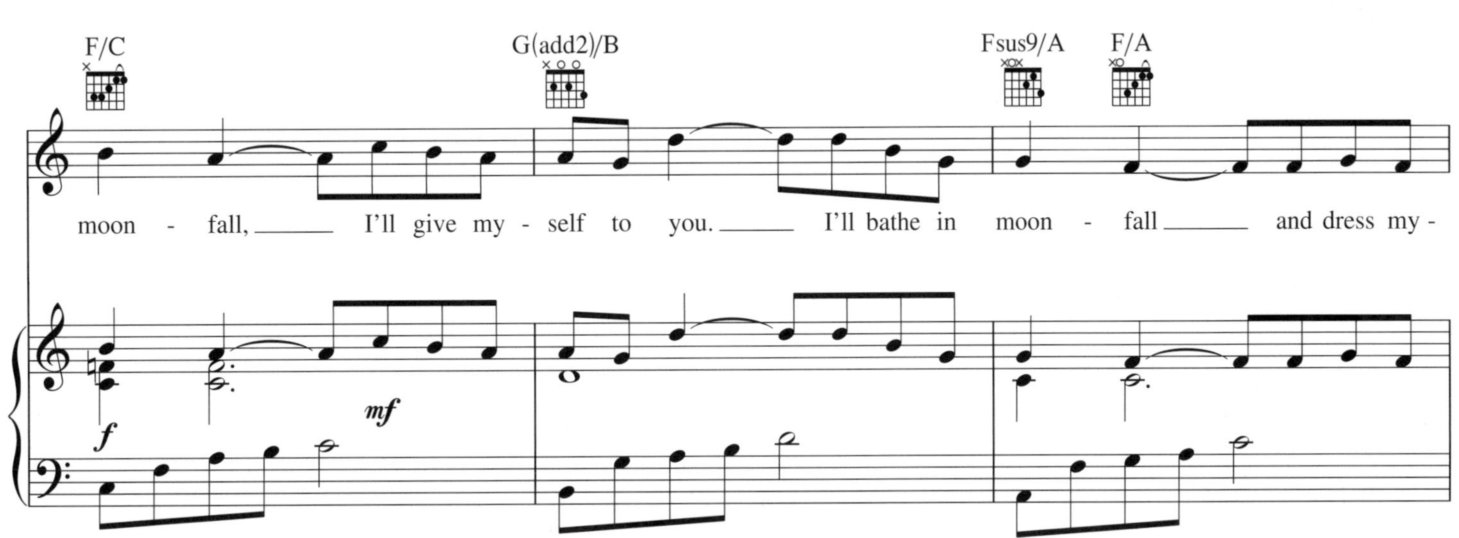

A tempo (less ad lib.)
Em
Am
Am9/G
5fr
self in dew. Be - fore the cloak of night re - veals the morn,
mf
Fmaj7
B7/E
E7/D
F/C
time hold its breath while it con - ceals the dawn, and in the moon - fall, all sound is
f
mf
G(add2)/B
Fsus9/A
F/A
Em
fro - zen still. Yet warm a - gainst me, your skin will warm the chill of
Fmaj7♯11
Fmaj7
D13
4fr
D7
F11
3fr
F7
G♯m/F♯
4fr
F♯maj7
moon - fall. I feel its fin - gers; lin - gers the veil of night - shade,
f

G(add♯4)/D G
E7
G
Esus
E
light made from stars that all-too - soon fall, moon - fall that pours from you.
ff
f
rit.
Am
Am9/G
5fr
Fmaj9
Be-twixt our hearts, let noth-ing in - ter- vene. Be-tween our eyes, the on - ly
a tempo
D/F♯
C6/G
E/G♯
Am
sight I've seen is lus - trous moon - fall as it blinds my view,
p sub.
mf
B♭/D
E♭/G
3fr
Am
Fm(maj7)
B♭(add♯4)/D
3fr
Am
so that soon I on - ly see but you.
rit.
f a tempo
fp

RIVER IN THE RAIN

from BIG RIVER

Words and Music by
ROGER MILLER

D
wind - in' some - place just tryin' to find the sun.
A7/E
Wheth-er the sun - shine, wheth-er the rain,
A7 G D G
riv-er, I love you just the same. But some-times in a time of trou-ble
D/F# Em7 D A7
when you're out of hand and your mud - dy bub - bles roll a-cross my

D
Em7
D/F♯
G
floor
car-ryin' way the things I treas-ure;
D/F♯
Em7
D
hell, there ain't no way to meas - ure why I love you more than I
A7
did the day be - fore.
Riv - er in the rain,
G
some-times at night you look like a

D
long white train
wind-in' your way a - way some-where.
wind-in' your way a - way from me.
To Coda
A7/E
A7
G
D
D.S. al Coda
Riv-er, I love you. Don't you care? But some-times in a
CODA
A7
G
D
A7/D
Gmaj7/D
A/D
Riv-er, I've nev - er seen the sea.
8va
p
D
A7/D
Gmaj7
A5
D5
8va

I DREAMED A DREAM
from LES MISÉRABLES

Music by CLAUDE-MICHEL SCHÖNBERG
Lyrics by ALAIN BOUBLIL,
JEAN-MARC NATEL and HERBERT KRETZMER

Cm7
E♭/B♭
A♭
A♭/G
3fr
6fr
4fr
die.
I dreamed that God would be for -
Fm7
B♭
E♭
E♭/D
3fr
giv - ing.
Then I was young and un - a -
Cm
E♭/B♭
A♭
A♭/G
3fr
6fr
4fr
fraid,
and dreams were made and used and
Fm7
B♭6
E♭
E♭/D
3fr
wast - ed.
There was no ran - som to be

Cm7
Eb/Bb
Ab
Ab/G
Fm7
Bb
paid, no song un - sung, no wine un - tast - ed.
C
C/E
Fm
C
C7
But the ti - gers come at night with their voic - es soft as
poco più mosso
F
F/A
Bb
Bb/D
Ebm
thun - der, as they tear your hope a - part,
Bb
Eb
Fm/Eb
Eb
Ab/Eb
as they turn your dream to shame.

B♭
E♭
3fr
E♭/D
He She slept a sum - mer by my
rall.
a tempo
Cm
3fr
E♭/B♭
6fr
A♭
4fr
A♭/G
Fm7
B♭6
side.
He She filled my days with end - less won - der.
E♭
3fr
E♭/D
Cm7
3fr
E♭/B♭
6fr
A♭
4fr
B♭6
He She took my child - hood in his her stride,
but he she was gone when au - tumn
E♭
3fr
B♭/D
B♭m6/D♭
2fr
C
came.
poco accel. e cresc.

F
F/E
Dm7
F/C
And still I dreamed he'd she'd come to me,
mf più mosso
Bb
Bb/A
Gm7
C
F
F/E
that we would live the years to - geth - er.
But there are dreams that can - not
Dm7
F/C
Bb
Bb/A
Gm7
C
be,
and there are storms we can - not weath - er.
cresc.
F
F/E
Dm7
F/C
I had a dream my life would
f
appassionato

B♭
B♭/A
Gm7
B♭/C
C
be
so dif - f'rent from this hell I'm
3
F
F/E
Dm7
F/C
liv - ing, so dif-f'rent now from what it seemed.
cresc.
ff
dim.
poco rall.
B♭
C
F
F/E
Now life has killed the dream I dreamed.
mp
p
a tempo
Dm7
F/A
B♭
C9
F
rall.

ALL I ASK OF YOU

from THE PHANTOM OF THE OPERA

Music by ANDREW LLOYD WEBBER
Lyrics by CHARLES HART
Additional Lyrics by RICHARD STILGOE

D♭maj7 G♭6/D♭ C♭ A♭/C
here, with you, be - side you, to guard you and to guide you.
D♭ B♭m7 E♭m7 A♭ D♭/F B♭m7
CHRISTINE:
Say you love me ev - ery wak - ing mo - ment, turn my head with talk of
E♭m7 E♭m7/A♭ D♭ B♭m7 E♭m7 A♭
sum - mer - time. Say you need me with you now and al - ways;
D♭/F G♭ D♭/A♭ E♭m/A♭ A♭6 E♭m7/A♭
prom - ise me that all you say is true, that's all I ask of
rit.

Db
RAOUL:
Dbmaj7
Gb6/Db
Let me be your shel - ter, let me be your light; you're safe, no one will find you your
you.
a tempo
mf
Cb
Ab/C
Db
CHRISTINE:
fears are far be - hind you. All I want is free - dom, a world with no more night; and
Dbmaj7
Gb6/Db
Cb
Ab/C
Db
Bbm7
RAOUL:
you, al - ways be - side me, to hold me and to hide me. Then say you'll share with me one
Ebm7
Ab
Db/F
Bbm7
Ebm7
G/Ab
Ab
Ab6
Ab7
love, one life - time; let me lead you from your sol - i - tude.

D♭
B♭m7
E♭m7
A♭
D♭/F
G♭
Say you need me with you, here beside you, an-y-where you go, let me go
D♭/A♭
E♭m7/A♭
A♭6
E♭m7/A♭
D♭
B♭m7
CHRISTINE:
too.
Chris-tine, that's all I ask of you.
Say you'll share with me one
rit.
molto rit.
a tempo
E♭m7
A♭
D♭/F
B♭m7
E♭m7
A♭
A♭7
love, one life-time; say the word and I will fol-low you.
D♭
B♭m7
E♭m7
A♭
D♭/F
G♭
TOGETHER:
Share each day with me, each night, each morn-ing.
CHRISTINE:
8vb
Say you love me!
RAOUL:
You know I
rit.

D♭/A♭
E♭m7/A♭
A♭6
E♭m7/A♭
D♭
B♭m7
RAOUL & CHRISTINE:
do.
Love me, that's all I ask of you.
molto rit.
a tempo
E♭m7
A♭
D♭/F
B♭m7
E♭m7
G/A♭
A♭
A♭6
A♭9
D♭
B♭m7
E♭m7
A♭
D♭/F
G♭
CHRISTINE & RAOUL:
An - y - where you go, let me go
f
ff largo
D♭/A♭
E♭m7/A♭
A♭6
E♭m7/A♭
D♭
RAOUL & CHRISTINE:
too; love me, that's all I ask of you.
mp
molto rit.

MR. MONOTONY
from JEROME ROBBINS' BROADWAY

Words and Music by
IRVING BERLIN

E♭ E♭/D♭ A♭6/C B7 B♭7sus E♭ E♭/D♭
Any pleasant interlude that would mean a
A♭6/C B7 B♭7sus E♭6 E♭6/G A♭m6 B♭9
change of mood didn't go with Mister Mo-
E♭ E♭/D♭ A♭6/C B7 B♭7sus A♭ A♭7/G♭
notony. Sometimes he would
D♭6/F E7 E♭7sus A♭ A♭7/G♭ D♭6/F E7 E♭7sus
change the key, but the same dull melody

A♭6
A♭6/C
D♭m6
E♭9
A♭
A♭7/G♭
would e - merge from Mis - ter Mo - not - o - ny.
D♭6/F
E7
E♭7sus
B♭
B♭7/A♭
E♭6/G
F♯7
F7sus
Folks for miles would run a - way.
B♭
B♭7/A♭
E♭6/G
F♯7
F7sus
B♭
Cm7
On - ly one pre - ferred to stay. She would come a -
C♯dim
B♭6
N.C.
round and say, "Have you got an - y mo - not - o - ny, to -

B♭7
E♭
E♭7/D♭
A♭6/C
B7
B♭7sus
day?" They got mar - ried as they should,
E♭
E♭/D♭
A♭6/C
B7
B♭7sus
E♭6
E♭6/G
and a - round the neigh - bor - hood, she was known as
A♭m6
B♭9
E♭
E♭7/D♭
A♭6/C
B7
B♭7sus
Mis - sus Mo - not - o - ny.
E♭
E♭7/D♭
A♭6/C
B7
B♭7sus
E♭
E♭7/D♭
They were hap - py as could be, and they raised a

A♭6/C
B7
B♭7sus
E♭6
E♭6/G
A♭m6
B♭9
fam - i - ly; six or sev - en lit - tle Mo -
E♭
E♭/D♭
A♭6/C
B7
B♭7sus
A♭
Fm7
not - o - nies. From an - oth - er vil - lage came a
B♭m7
D♭/E♭
E♭7
A♭
Fm7
snap - py clar - i - net - er. She heard him play and, strange to
B♭m7
D♭/E♭
E♭7
A♭6
A♭6/C
D♭m6
E♭9
say, she liked him bet - ter. 'Twas the end of Mis - ter Mo -

A♭
A♭/G♭
D♭6/F
E7
E♭7sus
B♭
B♭/A♭
not - o - ny.
She re - fused him
E♭6/G
F♯7
F7sus
B♭
B♭/A♭
E♭6/G
F♯7
F7sus
when he tried
bring - ing her back
to his side.
B♭
Cm7
C♯dim
B♭7/D
N.C.
She just an - swered
when he cried,
"Have you
E♭7
got an - y mo - not - o - ny to - day?"
"Have - n't

Fm7
B♭7
E♭
E♭/D♭
Cm7
E♭/B
B♭9♯5
got an - y mo - not - o - ny to - day.
Can't
E♭
E♭/D♭
Cm7
E♭/B
B♭9♯5
E♭
E♭/D♭
play
to - day.
Cm7
E♭/B
E♭/B♭
E♭m7
E9
Have - n't got an - y mo - not - o - ny to -
E♭
E♭/D♭
A♭6/C
B7
B♭7sus
E♭6
day."

WITH EVERY BREATH I TAKE

from CITY OF ANGELS

Music by CY COLEMAN
Lyrics by DAVID ZIPPEL

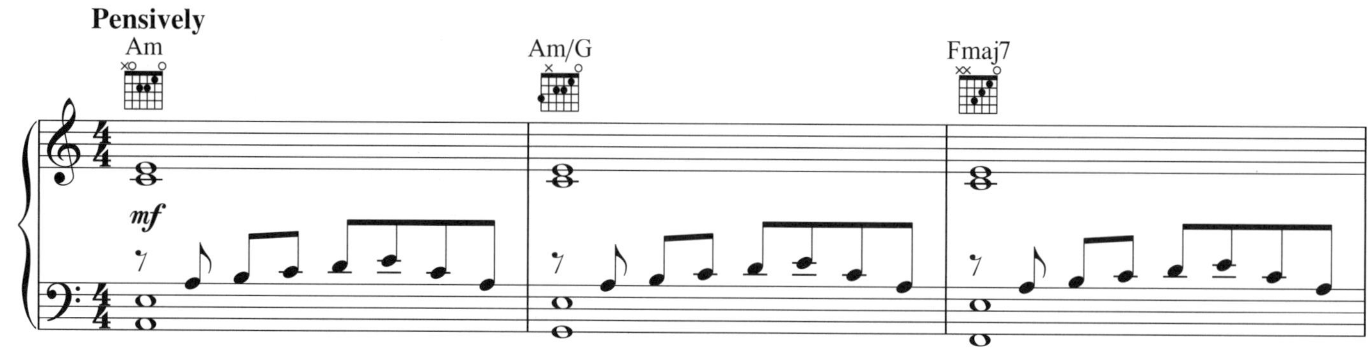

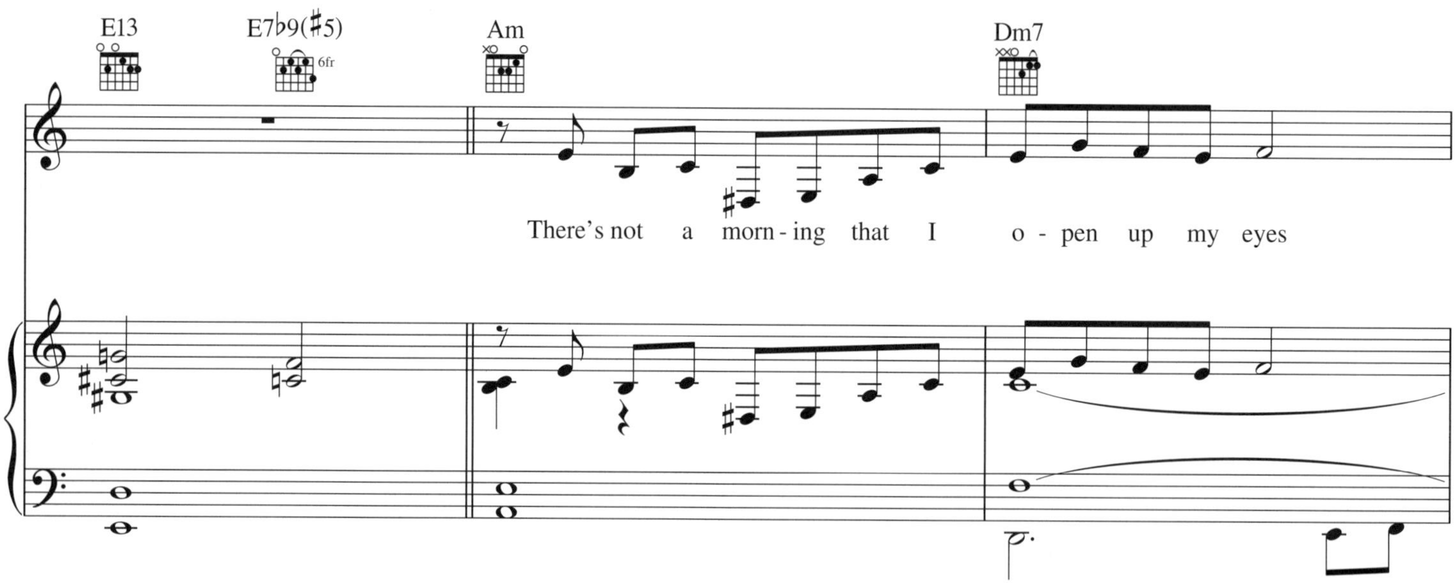

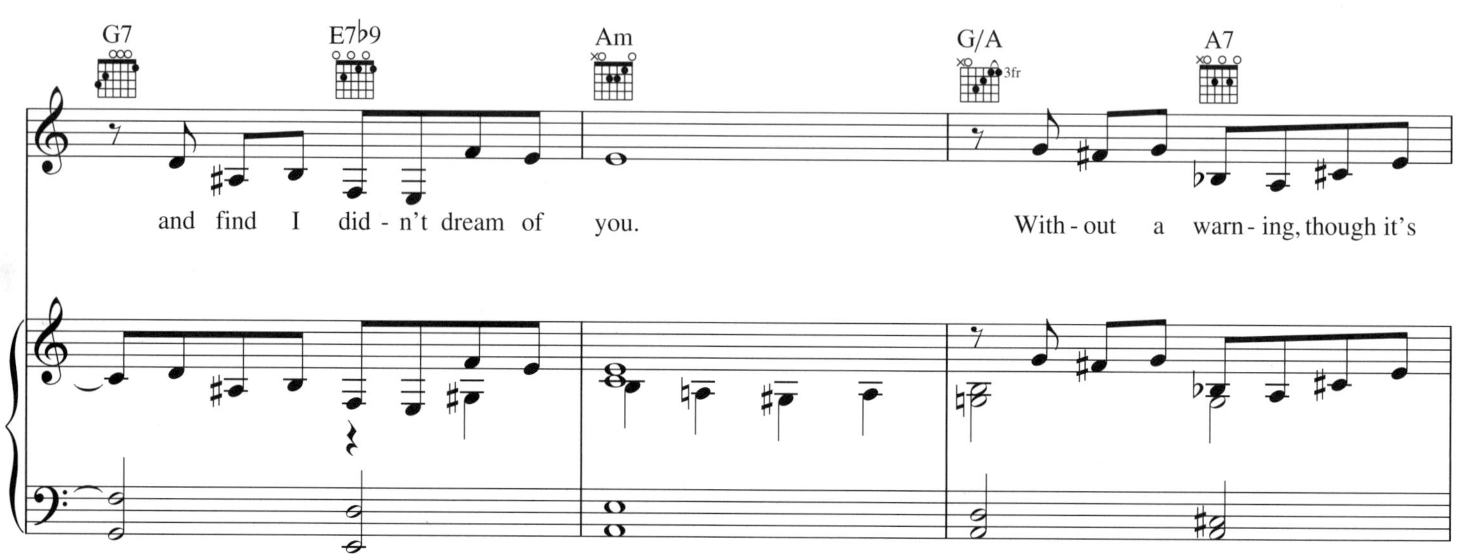

Dm9
3fr
Dm
Bm7♭5
B7♭9
E7sus
E7
never - er a sur - prise,
soon as I a - wake
thoughts of you a - rise
with
Am7
D9
4fr
ev - 'ry breath I take.
Am7
D9
4fr
Dm7
Dm7/C
At an - y
time
or
Bm7
E13
E7♯5
Am11
3fr
Am7
G6
C6/E
Fmaj9
place
I
close
my eyes and see your
face
and

Bm7♭5
E7♭9
Am7
I'm em - brac - ing you.
D9
4fr
F6/9
Fmaj7
B♭
If on - ly I be - lieved that dreams come
E♭
3fr
Dm6/E
E7♭9
Am
true. Dar - ling, you were the one who said for -
Dm7
G7
E7♭9
Am
ev - er from the start, and I've been drift - ing since you've gone,

G/A
3fr
A7
Dm9
3fr
Dm
G11
G13/F
3fr
G7/F
out on a lone - ly sea that on - ly you can chart.
I've been go - ing on
Cmaj7/E
C/E
Gm9
3fr
C9
Fmaj9
C/E
know - ing that my heart will break
E13♭9
B♭13
6fr
Am
with ev - 'ry breath I take.
Am/G
Fmaj7
E13
Am7

NEVER MET A MAN I DIDN'T LIKE

from THE WILL ROGERS FOLLIES

Music by CY COLEMAN
Lyrics by BETTY COMDEN and ADOLPH GREEN

C7
F6
F
Em7
A7
or
Bow - 'ry
bum,
yes, I've
come
a
or
work - ing
Joe,
though I
know
life's
C/D
D7♭9
4fr
Gm7
long
way
down the
pike,
one
long
rock - y
hike,
B♭/C
C7♭9
1
F
nev - er met a
man
I
did - n't
like.
Fmaj7
F7
B♭
C
B♭/D
C/E
Nev - er shook a

2
F
B♭
C
B♭/D
C/E
F
did - n't like.
In all of my wan -
F+
B♭
Gm
3fr
- d'rin',
I've bumped into all kinds of peo - ple;
Gm7/C
C7
F6
F
fan - cy cin - e - ma stars, fake e - van - gel - ists,
pol - i - ti - cians,
Em7
A7
C/D
D7♭9
4fr
mor - ti - cians,
And I have
reached the con - clu - sion,

Gm7
Bb/C
while hik - ing the pike.
Though I try and I try,
C7b9
F
Bb
C
Bb/D
C/E
nev - er once met a guy that I did - n't like.
I said I've roamed a - long the
F
F+
Bb
Gm
3fr
Na - pa Val - ley, Shu - bert Al - ley, Rue de la Paix,
Gm7/C
C7
F6
F
O - kla - ho - ma and Kal - a - ma - zoo.

Em7
A7
C/D
D7♭9
4fr
And I have reached the con - clu - sion,
Gm7
B♭/C
while mak - ing that hike,
yes, I'll say till I'm done,
C7♭9
F
B♭
C
B♭/D
C/E
no, I nev - er met one that I did - n't like.
F
F+
B♭
Met the worst and met the best,
some that put me

Gm
3fr
Gm7/C
C7
to the test,
al - most made me
change my mind.
F6
F
Em7
A7
C/D
Yet some - how I
al - ways find
if you don't ex -
D7♭9
4fr
Gm7
pect too much
there's a cer - tain
hu - man touch
B♭/C
C7♭9
F
ho - mo sa - pi - ens has got
oth - er an - i - mals

Db7
Gb
Gb+
have not.
Try the shoes on that are his,
mf
Cb
Abm
Abm7/Db
feel what makes him what he is,
what it's like in -
Db7
Gb6
Gb
Fm7
Bb7
side his skin,
liv - in' in the skin he's in.
Db/Eb
Eb7b9
Abm7
Just like me, a lump of sod,
there but for the

C♭/D♭
4fr
D♭7♭9
grace of God, that is the phi - los - o - phy of this
G♭
D7
G
part - time Cher - o - kee. Pres - i - dent and king
f
G+
3fr
C
Am
or Pat and Mike, folks can laugh but
Am7/D
D7
G6
G
I can't give up hope.

F♯m7
B7
D/E
E7♭9
Spun my rope a long way
Am7
C/D
down the pike, nev - er met a man
D7♭9
4fr
G
E♭
3fr
I did - n't like. High-toned gent,
G
E♭
3fr
G
Bow - 'ry bum, Prince of Wales, work - ing Joe,

E♭
3fr
G
E♭
3fr
Pat and Mike, Cher - o - kee phi - los - o - phy.
G
E♭7
G
Nev - er met a man I did - n't like.
rit.
a tempo
Gmaj7
G7
C
D
C/E
D/F♯
G
Gmaj7
G7
C
D
C/E
D/F♯
G
rall.

SOMEONE TO WATCH OVER ME

from CRAZY FOR YOU

Music and Lyrics by GEORGE GERSHWIN
and IRA GERSHWIN

C9
Fmaj7
Am7
D7
found him yet; he's the big af-fair I can - not for-get.
Dm7
Dm7/G
G7
C
F
On - ly man I ev - er think of with re - gret.
C
B7♭9
Em
A
I'd like to add his in - i - tial to my
Em
Em7
A7
G/B
Em7
mon - o - gram. Tell me,

Am7
D7
G
F
Em
G7
where is the shep - herd for this lost lamb?
rall.
C
C7
F6
Fdim7
C/E
E♭dim7
There's a some - bod - y I'm long - ing to see. I hope that he
a tempo
G7/D
C♯dim7
Dm
A7/E
Dm/F
F♯m7♭5
4fr
F/G
G7
turns out to be some - one who'll watch o - ver
C
E7♯5
F
G7
C
C7
me. I'm a lit - tle lamb who's

F6
Fdim7
C/E
E♭dim7
G7/D
C♯dim7
lost in the wood. I know I could al - ways be good
Dm
A7/E
Dm/F
F♯m7♭5
4 fr
F/G
G7
C
C7
F
G7
to one who'll watch o - ver me.
C
F
Al - though he may not be the man some girls
C
B7
think of as hand - some, to my heart he

E7
A
A7
D7
G7
car - ries the key.
C
C7
F
Fdim7
C/E
E♭dim7
Won't you tell him please to put on some speed,
fol - low my lead,
G7/D
C♯dim7
Dm
A7/E
Dm/F
F♯m7♭5
4 fr
F/G
G7
oh, how I need some - one to watch o - ver
1
C
C7
F
E7
Dm7
G7♯5
me.
2
C
C7
F
Fm
C
me.

LOVING YOU
from PASSION

Music and Lyrics by
STEPHEN SONDHEIM

Ebmaj9
Eb(add9)/G
F7
Abmaj7#11
3fr
gives me pur - pose, gives me voice to say to the world:
Ab6/Gb
4fr
this is why I live. You are why I
mp
Cmaj9
C6
Cmaj9
live. Lov - ing you is
Am9
5fr
why I do the things I do.

Dm11
D7
Dm11
Fmaj7
Lov - ing you is not in my con - trol.
cresc.
B♭maj7♯11
But lov - ing you, I have a goal, for what's
F(add2)/A
Am
Dm7
D7
Gm9
left of my life.
I will live, and
p
Gm
C7sus
F
F/C
I would die for you.

KISS OF THE SPIDER WOMAN

from KISS OF THE SPIDER WOMAN

Words by FRED EBB
Music by JOHN KANDER

C♯m
G♯7
C♯m
G♯7
bed - room, the par - lor, or e - ven the street. There's
C♯m
F♯
C♯m
F♯
no place on earth you're like - ly to miss
G♯7sus
her kiss.
cresc.
G♯7
C♯m
C♯sus
Soon - er or lat - er, in
mp

C♯m
C♯9sus
C♯m
C♯sus
4fr
sun - light or gloom, when the red can - dles flick - er she'll
C♯m
C♯9sus
C♯m
F♯
walk in the room and the cur - tain will shake and the
C♯m
F♯
fire will hiss. Here comes her
G♯7sus
G♯9
5fr
kiss. And the
cresc.
rall. poco a poco

C♯m
C♯m/B
D♯7/A♯
F♯m/A
G♯7
4fr
6fr
moon grows dim - mer at the
f marc.
a tempo
tide's low ebb and her
F♯m6/A
black beads shim - mer and you're
G♯7sus
ach - ing to move, but you're caught in the web of the
rall.

C♯m
C♯m/B
D♯7/A♯
F♯m/A
G♯7
Spi - der Wom-an with her
a tempo
C♯m
C♯m/B
D♯7/A♯
F♯m6/A
vel - vet cape. You can
C♯m/G♯
F♯m
C♯m
G♯7sus
G♯7
scream, but you can - not es -
rall. poco a poco
colla voce
C♯m9
G♯7
C♯m9
G♯7
cape.
p a tempo

C♯m7
G♯7
C♯m9
G♯7
4fr
f
C♯m
G♯7
C♯m
G♯7
Soon - er or lat - er your love will ar - rive and he
mp staccato
C♯m
G♯7
C♯m
G♯7
touch - es your heart. You're a - lert and a - live. And there's
C♯m
F♯
C♯m
F♯
on - ly one pin that can punc - ture such bliss:

G♯7sus
4fr
her
kiss.
poco cresc.
G♯7
4fr
C♯m
4fr
C♯9sus
4fr
Soon - er or lat - er you
f
mp
C♯m
C♯9sus
C♯m
C♯9sus
bathe in suc - cess and your min - ions sa - lute. They say
C♯m
C♯9sus
C♯m
F♯
noth - ing but "yes." But your pow - er is emp - ty. It

C♯m
F♯
fades like the mist
once you've been
G♯7sus
G♯7
kissed.
And the
cresc.
rall. poco a poco
C♯m
C♯m/B
D♯7/A♯
F♯m6/A
moon grows dim - mer
at the
f marc.
a tempo
C♯m
C♯m/B
D♯7/A♯
tide's low ebb.
And your

F#m6/A
G#7
C#m
C#m/B
breath comes fast - er and you're
D#7/A#
F#m6/A
G#7sus
G#7
ach - ing to move, but you're caught in the web of the
cresc. e rall.
C#
C#/B
F#6/A#
F#m/A
G#7
Spi - der Wom - an in her
ff a tempo
C#
C#/B
F#/A#
F#m/A
vel - vet cape. You can
rall.

C♯m/G♯
G♯7
run, you can scream, you can
cresc. poco a poco
Maestoso
E/G♯
F♯m/G♯
hide, but you can - not es -
C♯m9
G♯m7♭5
cape.
ff a tempo
C♯m
sfz

WITH ONE LOOK

from SUNSET BOULEVARD

Music by ANDREW LLOYD WEBBER
Lyrics by DON BLACK and CHRISTOPHER HAMPTON,
with contributions by AMY POWERS

Bm7
D/E
E7/D
A/C♯
Em7
or the love that you've hun - gered for. When I speak it's with my
A
D
A/E
E7
A
E7/A
soul, I can play an - y role. No words can tell the
A
E7/A
D
A/C♯
Bm7
E
sto - ries my eyes tell, watch me when I frown, you can't write that down. You
C
G/C
C
G
A
F♯m7
A/E
know I'm right, it's there in black and white, when I look your way you'll hear

Bm7
E
A
F♯m
what I say. Yes, with one look I put words to shame,
Bm7
E
E7/D
A/C♯
Em7
just one look sets the screen a-flame. Si - lent mu-sic starts to
A
D
A/C♯
Bm7
E7
play, one tear in my eye makes the whole world cry.
A
F♯m
Bm7
With one look they'll for - give the past, they'll re - joice I've re -
f

D/E
E7/D
A/C♯
Em/B
A/C♯
D
turned at last to my peo-ple in the dark,
A/E
E7
A
D
Bm
still out there in the dark.
f
Em7
G/A
3fr
A
D/F♯
Am
Si - lent mu-sic starts to
p
D
G
D/F♯
Em7
A
play. With one look you'll know all you need to know.
mf

B/F#
G#m
C#m
C#m/B
With one look I'll ig - nite a blaze, I'll re - turn to my
E/F#
F#/E
B/D#
F#m7
B
glo - ry days. They'll say Nor - ma's back at last.
E(add2)
E6
A
This time I am stay - ing, I'm stay - ing for good, I'll be back where I was born to
rit.
Emaj7
E/F#
B
be, with one look I'll be me.
molto rit.
ff a tempo

SEASONS OF LOVE

from RENT

Words and Music by
JONATHAN LARSON

B♭sus2 Am7 Gm7 C7sus F C Dm Am B♭sus2 Am7
day-lights, in sun-sets, in mid-nights, in cups of cof-fee, in inch-es, in miles, in
Gm7 C7sus Dm Am B♭sus2 Am7 Gm7 C7sus F C Dm Am
laugh-ter, in strife, in five hun-dred twen-ty-five thou-sand six hun-dred min - utes. How
B♭sus2 Am7 Gm7 C7sus Dm Am E♭/B♭ B♭
6fr
do you meas-ure a year in the life? How a-bout love?
B♭/F F E♭/B♭ B♭ Dm/C C
6fr
How a-bout love? How a-bout

E♭/B♭
B♭
Gm/F
F
E♭(add2)
love? ___
Meas-ure in love.
C9sus
B♭sus2
Am7
Gm7 C7sus
F
C Dm Am
Sea - sons of love, ___ sea - sons of
B♭sus2
Am7
Gm7 C7sus
Dm
Am B♭sus2
Am7
love. ___
Five hun-dred twen-ty-five thou-sand
Gm7 C7sus
F
C Dm Am B♭sus2
Am7
Gm7 C7sus
Dm
Am
six hun - dred min - utes,
five hun-dred twen-ty-five thou-sand jour-neys to plan. _

B♭sus2 Am7 Gm7 C7sus F C Dm Am B♭sus2 Am7
Five hun-dred twen-ty-five thou-sand six hun-dred min - utes. How do you meas-ure the life of a
Gm7 C7sus Dm Am B♭sus2 Am7 Gm7 C7sus F C Dm Am
wom-an or a man? In truth that she learned or in times that he cried, in
B♭sus2 Am7 Gm7 C7sus Dm Am B♭sus2 Am7
bridg - es he burned or the way that she died. It's time now to sing out, though the
Gm7 C7sus F C Dm Am B♭sus2 Am7 Gm7 C7sus Dm Am
sto - ry nev - er ends. Let's cel - e-brate, re-mem - ber a year in the life of friends. Re-mem-ber the

E♭/B♭
B♭
B♭/F
F
E♭/B♭
B♭
6fr
love,
re-mem-ber the
love,
Dm/C
C
E♭/B♭
B♭
Gm/F
F
re-mem-ber the
love,
meas-ure in
E♭(add2)
C9sus
B♭sus2
Am7
love.
8va
Sea - sons of
love,
Gm7
C7sus
F
C
Dm
Am
B♭sus2
Am7
Gm7
C7sus
Dm
sea - sons of
love.

NO MOON

from TITANIC

Music and Lyrics by
MAURY YESTON

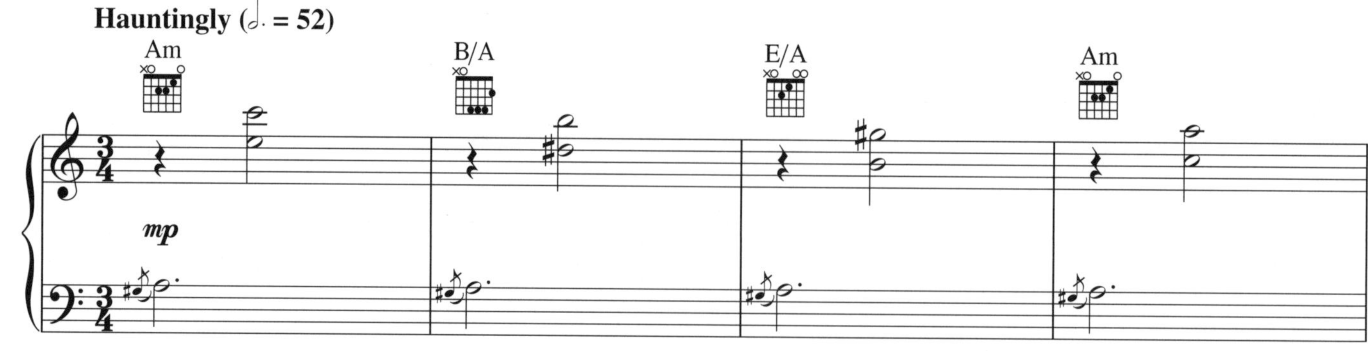

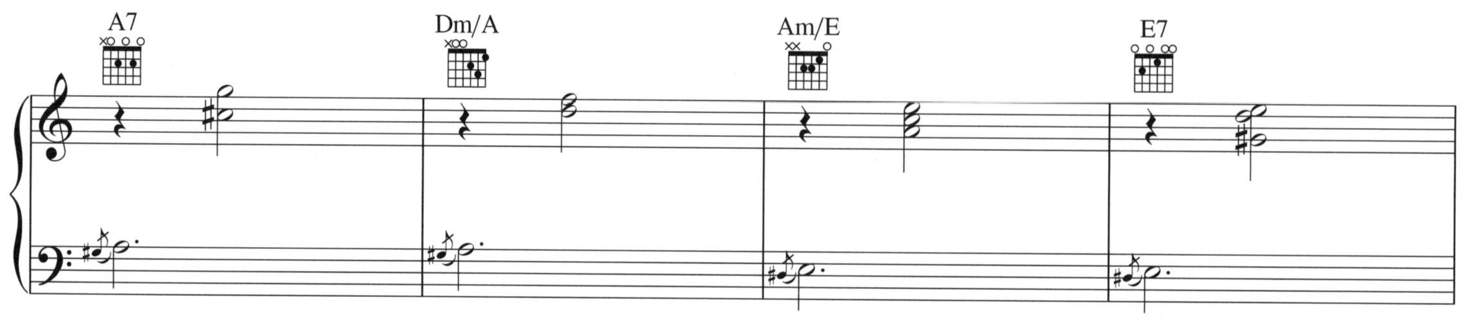

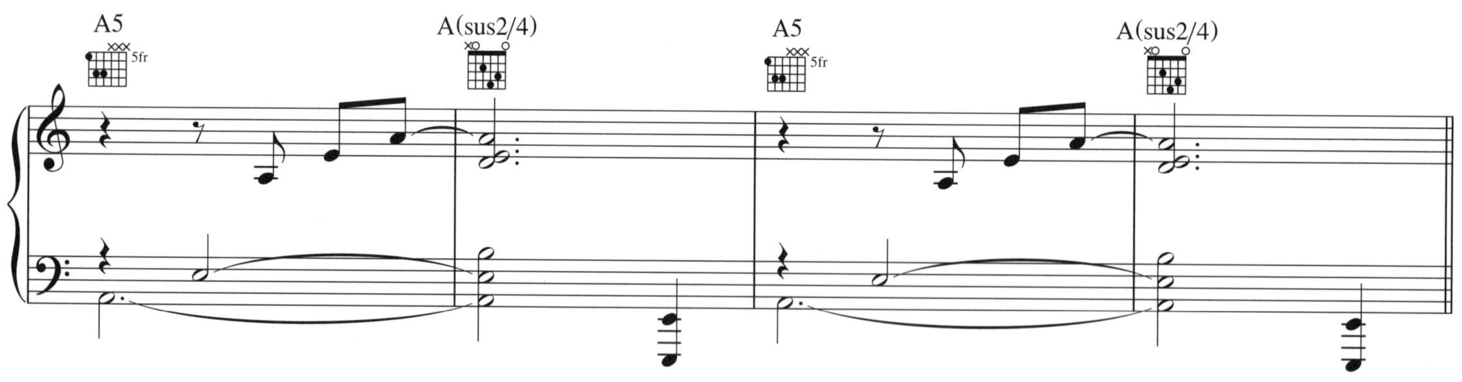

Bm7♭5
Em7
noth - ing to spy things by.
Fmaj9
Fmaj7/C
Dm11
3fr
Dm
No wave, no swell,
Bm7♭5
E7sus
E7
no line where sea meets sky.
G/A
3fr
Am/E
G/F
F/C
Still - ness, dark - ness.

Dm7
G7
C
Fmaj9
"Can't see a thing," says I. No re -
Bm7♭5
G♯dim7
Am
F♯m7♭5
4fr
flec - tion, not a shad - ow, not a
B♭
Am/E
E7
Am
A(sus2/4)
glint of light meets the eye.
A5
5fr
A(sus2/4)
A
Asus
And we go sail - ing,

Em7
C/E
Dm7
Bm7♭5/D
E
sail - ing ev - er west - ward
Am
Fmaj7
G7
on the sea. We go sail - ing,
C
F
Bm7♭5
Am/E
E7
sail - ing, ev - er on go
Am
B/A
E/A
Am
we...
mp

A7
Dm/A
Am/E
E7
To Coda
A5
A(sus2/4)
A5
A(sus2/4)
A -
Dm6/A
Am(add2)
head we plow
Dm/A
Am(add2)
in - to the dark - en - ing night. Can't

G9
9fr
Am(add2)
see the bow... How then to
cresc.
Fmaj7♯5
Fdim7
Am/E
Esus
search with on - ly
Fmaj9
E7♭9
D.S. al Coda
star - light?
CODA
A5
5fr
A(sus2/4)
Am
poco rit.

CIRCLE OF LIFE

Disney Presents THE LION KING: THE BROADWAY MUSICAL

Music by ELTON JOHN
Lyrics by TIM RICE

D
Bm
Em
found. But the sun roll - ing high through the sap-phire sky keeps great and
cresc.
C
A7sus
A7
D
small on the end - less round. It's the cir - cle of life
f
C/D
and it moves us all through de - spair and
G
Asus
hope, through faith and love.

A
D/F♯
B
Till we find our place,
on the path un - wind-
Em
Gm6/B♭
D/A
- ing,
in the cir - cle,
A
A7
G/D
D
the cir - cle of life.
p
D
Em7/D
A/C♯

D
Bm
Em7
C
Asus
A
D
Em7/D
A/C♯
D
Bm
cresc.
Em7
C
Asus
A7
D
RAFIKI & CHORUS:
It's the cir - cle of life
f
C/D
and it moves us all
through de - spair and

G
Asus
hope,
through faith and love.
A
F
D7/F♯
D7
Till we find our place
on the path un - wind-
ff
Gm
B♭m6/D♭
F/C
3fr
2fr
- ing,
in the cir - cle,
Csus
C7
B♭/F
F
the cir - cle of life.

RAZZLE DAZZLE

from FOSSE

Words by FRED EBB
Music by JOHN KANDER

F
F6/A
D♭7
4fr
C7
Give 'em the old ho - cus po - cus. Bead and feath - er 'em.
F7
How can they see with se - quins in their
B♭
eyes?
What if your hing - es
B♭m/G
F/C
G9/D
9fr
all are rust - ing? What if in fact you're just dis - gust - ing?

F/C
C7
F
Raz - zle daz - zle 'em and they'll nev - er catch wise.
(snap)
D
E♭
C7
F
D
E♭
C7
(snap)
(snap)
(snap)
F
Fdim
C7
Give 'em the old raz - zle daz - zle. Raz - zle daz - zle 'em.
mf
C♯dim
Give 'em a show that's so splen - dif - er - ous,

Dm7
G7
C7
F
row af - ter row will grow vo - cif - er - ous. Give 'em the old
F♯dim
9fr
C7
flim flam flum - mox. Fool and frac - ture 'em.
F7
B♭
How can they hear the truth a - bove the roar.
B♭m/G
Throw'em a fake and a fi - na - gle.

F/C
G9/D
9fr
F/C
They'll nev - er know you're just a ba - gel.
Raz - zle daz - zle 'em
C7
F
D
E♭
3fr
C7
and they'll beg you for more.
(snap)
(snap)
Adim
E♭9/B♭
5fr
E♭7
A♭
4fr
A♭/C
3fr
C♭dim
Give 'em the old raz - zle daz - zle.
Give 'em the old raz - zle daz - zle.
(snap)
(snap)
E♭7/B♭
6fr
E♭7
Raz - zle daz - zle 'em.
Raz - zle daz - zle 'em.
Back since the days of
Give 'em an act that's

Edim
Fm
B♭7
E♭7
3fr
old Me - thu - se - lah, ev - 'ry - one loves the big bam - boo - za - la.
un - as - sail - a - ble, they'll wait a year 'til you're a - vail - a - ble.
A♭
4fr
E♭7
Give'em the old three ring cir - cus. Stun and stag - ger 'em.
Give'em the old dou - ble wham - my. Daze and diz - zy 'em.
8va
A♭7
4fr
D♭
When you're in trou - ble go in - to your dance.
Show 'em the first rate sor - cer - er you are.
(8va)
loco
B♭m7♭5
Though you are stiff - er than a gird - er,
Long as you keep 'em way off bal - ance,

1
2
A♭/E♭
B♭9/F
E♭7
A♭
4fr
Fdim/E♭
D♭/E♭
E♭9
F/A
B♭+
they'll let you get a - way with mur - der.
how can they spot you got no tal - ents.
Raz zle daz-zle 'em, and you got a ro -
mance.
Raz - zle daz - zle 'em,
raz - zle daz - zle 'em, raz - zle daz - zle 'em, and they'll make you a
star.
(snap)
mf
mp
cresc.
fz
f
3

YOU'RE NOBODY 'TIL SOMEBODY LOVES YOU

featured in the Broadway Musical CONTACT

Words and Music by RUSS MORGAN, LARRY STOCK and JAMES CAVANAUGH

Am D7 G6 D7#5
no - bod- y 'til some - bod- y cares. You
Bm7 B♭dim Am7
may be king, you may pos - sess the world and its gold, but
A6/9 A9#5 A9 Am7 D7 Am7 D7 D7#5
5fr 5fr
gold won't bring you hap - pi - ness when you're grow-ing old. The
G B7 E7♭9 E7 B7/F# E7/G#
world still is the same, you'll nev- er change it, as
3

Am
E7
Am
E7/B
sure as the stars shine a - bove.
Am/C
C
C♯dim7
You're no - bod - y 'til some - bod - y loves
G
E7
Am
E7/B
Am/C
A7
D7
you, so find your - self some - bod - y to
R.H.
1
2
G
F13sus
F9
E♭7sus
E♭7
D9
G
Cm7
G6
6fr
4fr
3fr
love. You're love.
L.H.

'TIL HIM
from THE PRODUCERS

Music and Lyrics by
MEL BROOKS

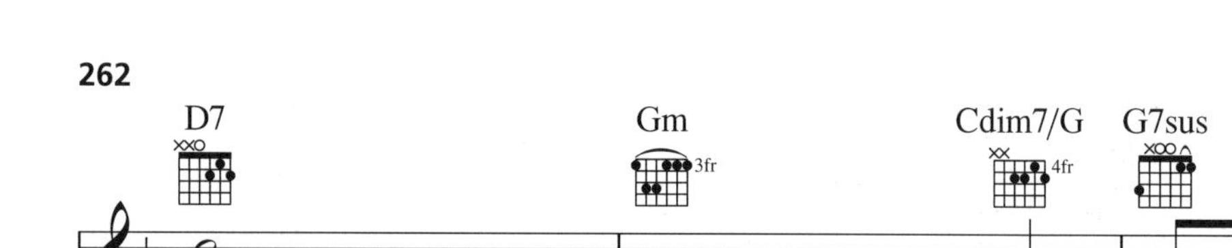
D7
Gm
3fr
Cdim7/G
4fr
G7sus
G7
C7
chance, then I felt his mag - ic and my heart be - gan to dance!
Gm7/C
C13
2fr
F
B♭/F
C7
Fmaj7
I was al - ways fright - ened, fraught with wor - ry 'til him.
mp
C7/F
F(add9)
C7/F
Am7♭5
I was go - ing no - where in a hur - ry 'til him.
D7
B♭
Gm7♭5
He filled up my emp - ty life,
5
f

Am7 Am7/D D7 G7sus G7 B♭/C Gm7♭5/C

filled it to the brim. There could nev - er ev - er be an - oth - er one like

poco rit. *mp* a tempo poco rit.

F C7 F F♯m7/B

him.

B9 E A/E B7/E

MAX:

No one ev - er ev - er real - ly knew me 'til

mp

E(add9) A/E B7 E B7/E B7/A

him. Ev - 'ry - one was al - ways out to screw me 'til

G♯m7♭5
C♯7♭5
8fr
C♯7
F♯m7
him.
Nev - er met a man I ev - er
B7
G♯m7
4fr
C♯7
trust - ed,
al - ways dealt with shy - sters in the past.
F♯m7
Fdim7
F♯7sus
F♯
B7sus
2fr
Now I'm well - ad - just - ed 'cause I've got a friend at last.
poco rit.
A tempo
B9
C9
Fmaj7
B♭/F
C7/F
Al - ways play - ing sin - gles, nev - er dou - bles 'til
poco rall.
mp

F
B♭/F
C/F
3fr
F(add9)
C7/F
him.
Nev - er had a pal to share my trou - bles 'til
Am7♭5
D7
Gm7
B♭m
LEO & MAX:
him.
He filled up my emp - ty life,
Am7
Am7/D
D7
G7sus
G7
Gm7♭5
LEO:
filled it to the brim.
There could nev - er ev - er be an - oth - er one
poco rit.
a tempo
poco rit.
Slowly
F
B♭/F
F(add9)
like him.

FORGET ABOUT THE BOY

from THOROUGHLY MODERN MILLIE

F/C
C9♯5
Tacet
F
C+
cross - er. For - get a - bout the boy.
Pull the plug.
hal - le - luh!
(mf)
F
B♭
F+
B♭
B♭m6
Ain't he the one who pulled the rug?
Now me and Mis - ter Wrong are through.
He's low - er than an
I'll find my - self an -
F/C
C+
Am7♭5
al - ley cat, dirt - y rat, and I flat -
oth - er beau who I know is no rov -
D7♯5
G9
C7
C7/B♭
ter.
er.
For - get a - bout the boy.

Am7♭5
D7
G9
For - get a - bout the boy. For - get a - bout
C7
C7♯5
F
F7/A
A♭°7
Gm7♭5
F
Tacet
the boy. And in the moon -
Dm6
B♭7
A7
Dm6
- light, don't you think a - bout him.
B♭7
A7
Dm6
B♭7
A7
Sis - ter, you're much bet - ter off with - out

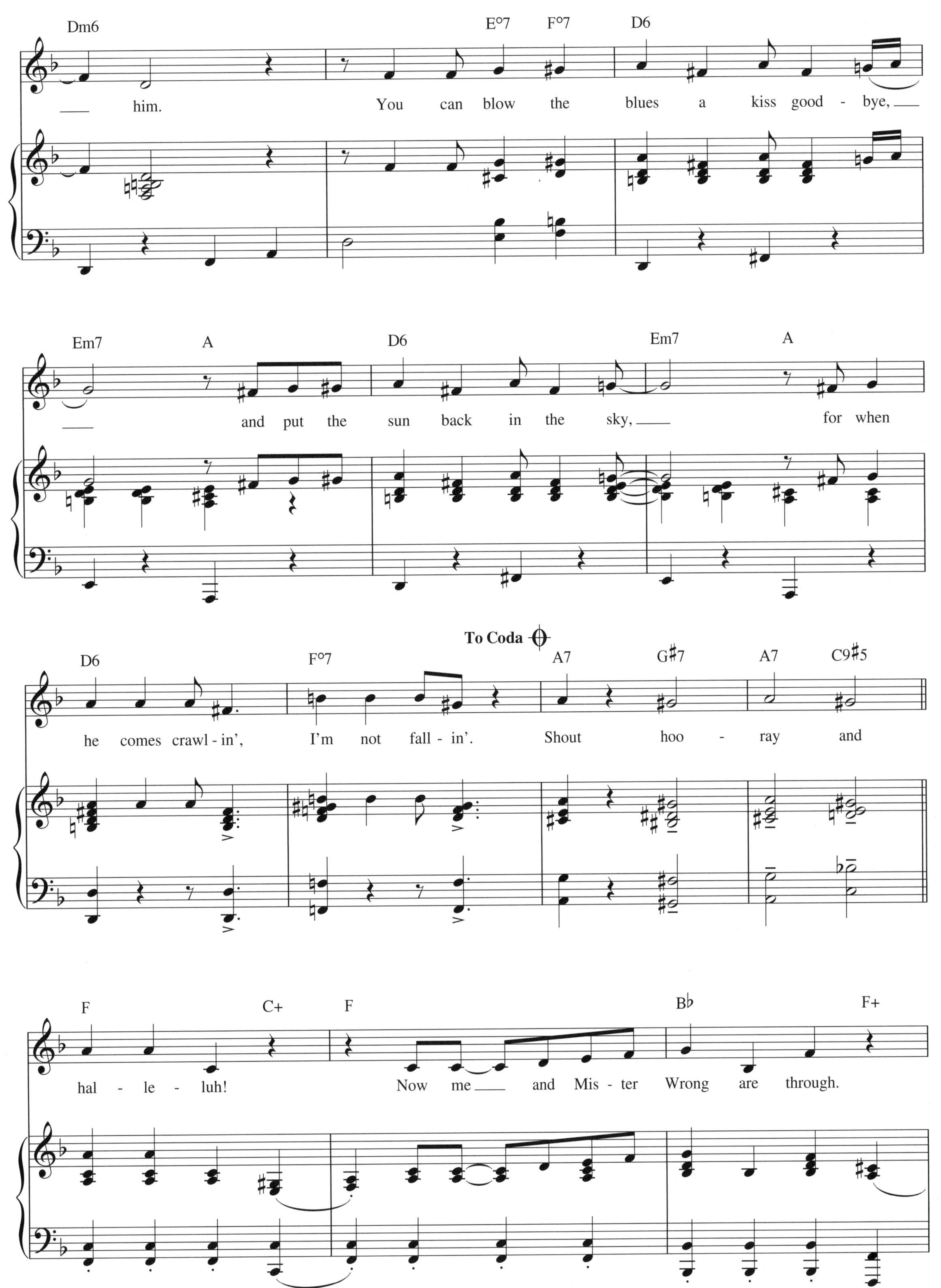

Dm6
E°7
F°7
D6
him.
You can blow the blues a kiss good - bye,
Em7
A
D6
Em7
A
and put the sun back in the sky,
for when
To Coda
D6
F°7
A7
G♯7
A7
C9♯5
he comes crawl - in', I'm not fall - in'. Shout hoo - ray and
F
C+
F
B♭
F+
hal - le - luh! Now me and Mis - ter Wrong are through.

B♭
B♭m6
F/C
C+
I'll find my-self an-oth-er beau who I know is no
Am7♭5
D7♯5
G9
C7
C7/B♭
rov-er.
For-get a-bout the boy.
Am7♭5
D7
G9
C7
For-get a-bout the boy.
For-get a-bout...
Tacet
F7
B♭/F
Jim-my, oh, Jim-my, Hor-ace, Dan-ny,
mp

D♭7
Mil - ton,
Vi - to Car - bo -
Per - cy, Ed - gar, Tim - o - thy, Al - fred, Per - cy, Ed - gar,
Jim - my,
Hor - ace
Ben - ja - min Pratt the
Ted - dy Mor - gan, Ted - dy Mor - gan,
cresc.
F/C
D7♯5
ne,
Bar - ney Schrei - ber, C. P.
Tim - o - thy, Al - fred.
Dan - ny, Mil - ton.
Third.
Ted - dy Mor - gan, Ted - dy Mor - gan.
f marc.

D7
G6
G
A.!
Jim - my, oh, Jim - my,
Cut the cord.
Is that the man I
mf

Am/G
Cm/G
G6
sil - ly boy.
Gee, what a
once a - dored?
He's noth - ing but an
al - ba - tross, no great

D7♯5
G6
D7♯5
Tacet
real swell guy!
For - get a - bout the boy.
loss, dou - ble - cross - er.
For - get a - bout the boy.

G6
C6
Jim - my, oh, Jim - my, oh, what
Pull the plug. Ain't he the one who pulled the rug?
Cm6
G6
D7♯5
joy! He makes my
He's low - er than an al - ley cat, dirt - y rat, and I
Dm6/F
E7♯5
A9
D7
D7/C
trou - bles fly. For - get a - bout the boy.
flat - ter.
cresc.
f

Bm7♭5
E7
A9
D7
For - get a - bout the boy. For - get a - bout the
N.C.
Dm6
boy!
B♭9
A9
Dm
D.S. al Coda
A7
G♯7
A7
C7♯5
Shout hoo - ray and

CODA
A7
G♯7
A7
B♭7
G♭/D♭
Hal - le - lu - jah!
f
A♭9
D♭7
D♭7/C♭
B♭m7♭5
E♭7
For - get a - bout the boy. For - get a - bout the boy.
A♭9 Tacet
G♭
G♭/F♭
For - get a - bout the boy!
G♭/E♭
G♭/D♭
C♭
N.C.
G♭

MAMA, I'M A BIG GIRL NOW

from HAIRSPRAY

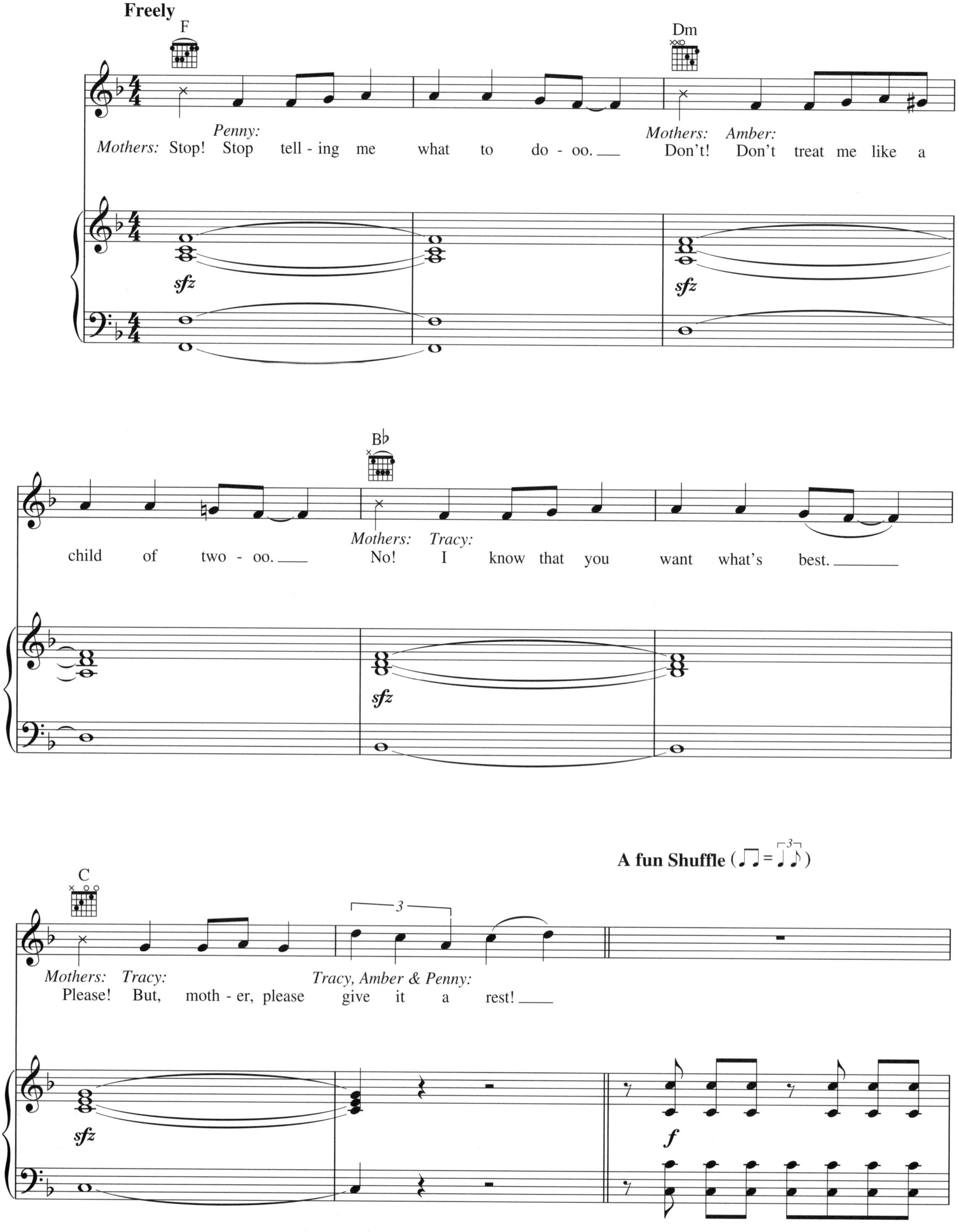

Freely

F Dm

Mothers: Stop! *Penny:* Stop tell - ing me what to do - oo. *Mothers:* Don't! *Amber:* Don't treat me like a

sfz sfz

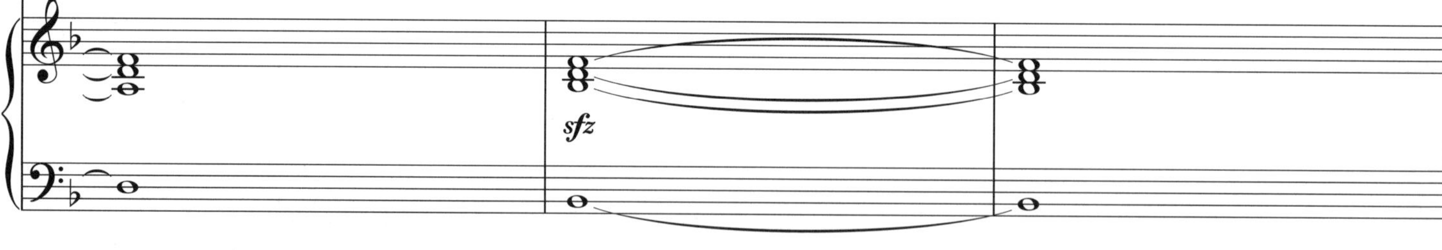

F
Dm
Mothers:
Mothers: Stop! Don't! No! Girls: Please! Stop! Don't!
mf
Bb
Mothers:
No! Girls: Please! Stop! Don't! No! Girls: Please!
C
C7
F
C
F
Ma - ma, I'm a big girl now! Tracy: Once up - on a time when I was
f
mp
Dm
just a kid, you nev - er let me do just what the old - er kids did. But

B♭
C
C7
F
lose that laun-dry list of what you won't al-low, 'cause, ma-ma, I'm a big girl now!
f
C
F
Amber: Once up-on a time I used to play with toys, but
mp
Dm
B♭
now I'd rath-er play a-round with teen-age boys. So, if I get a hick-ey, please don't
C
C7
F
F7
have a cow, 'cause, ma-ma, I'm a big girl now! Penny: Ma,
mf

B♭
F
___ I got - ta tell you that with - out a doubt I get my best danc - ing les - sons from you -
B♭
- oo. ___ You're ___ the one who taught me how to "Twist and Shout" ___ be - cause you
G
Dm/C
C
Dm/C
C
shout non - stop and you're so twist - ed ___ too - oo! Wo - oh - oh - oh - oh!
f
F
Dm
Tracy: Once I used to fid - get 'cause I just sat home. ___ Amber: But now I'm just like Gid - get and I
mf

B♭
Tracy:
Amber:
got - ta get to Rome! Penny: So, say ar - ri - ve - der - ci! Too - dle - oo! And ciao! Girls: 'Cause,
C
C7
F
D♭
G♭
ma - ma, I'm a big girl now! All: Oh - oh - oh! Stop! Don't!
f
E♭m
6fr
No! Please! Stop! Don't! No! Please!
C♭
D♭
D♭7
4fr
G♭
Stop! Don't! No! Please! Ma - ma, I'm a big girl now!

D♭ G♭
Chorus: Hey, ma - ma, say, ma - ma. Tracy: Once up - on a time I was a shy young thing. Could
mf
E♭m G♭7 C♭
bare - ly walk and talk so much as dance and sing. But let me hit the stage, I wan - na
D♭ D♭7 G♭ D♭
take my bow, 'cause, ma - ma, I'm a big girl now! Amber: Wo - oh - oh - oh - oh!
3
f
G♭ E♭m
Once up - on a time I used to dress up "Ken," but now that I'm a wom - an I like
mf

C♭
big - ger men! And I don't need a Bar - bie doll to show me how, 'cause,
D♭ D♭7 G♭ B♭m/A♭ G♭7/B♭ C♭
4fr 6fr 4fr
ma - ma, I'm a big girl now! Girls: Ma, you al - ways taught me what was
f
G♭
right from wrong, and now I just wan - na give it a try - y. Ma -
C♭ A♭
4fr
- ma, I've been in the nest for far too long. So please give a push and, ma - ma,

E♭m/D♭
D♭
E♭m/D♭
D♭
D
watch me fly!
Amber: Watch me fly!
Chorus: Hey, mama, say, mama.
G
Penny: One day I will meet a man you
won't condemn.
Em
Amber: And we will have some kids and you can
tor - ture them.
C
Tracy: But let me be a star be - fore I take that vow,
Girls: 'cause,
ff
mf

D
D7
G
D/F♯
Em
Em/D
C
D7
G
ma - ma, I'm a big girl now!
Oh - oh - oh!
Ma - ma, I'm a big girl now!
D/F♯
Em
Em/D
C6
D7
Amber: Hey - hey - hey - hey - hey!
Girls: Ma - ma, I'm a big girl!
G
Amber: Ooh, such a big, big girl! I'm a big girl now!
All: Stop! Don't!

Em
Oh - oh - oh - oh - oh.
No! Please! Stop! Don't!
C
Oh - oh - oh - oh.
No! Please! Stop! Don't!
D
D7
G
Please! Ma - ma, I'm a big girl now!
No! Please! Ma - ma, I'm a big girl now!
ff

PURPOSE

from the Broadway Musical AVENUE Q

Music and Lyrics by ROBERT LOPEZ
and JEFF MARX

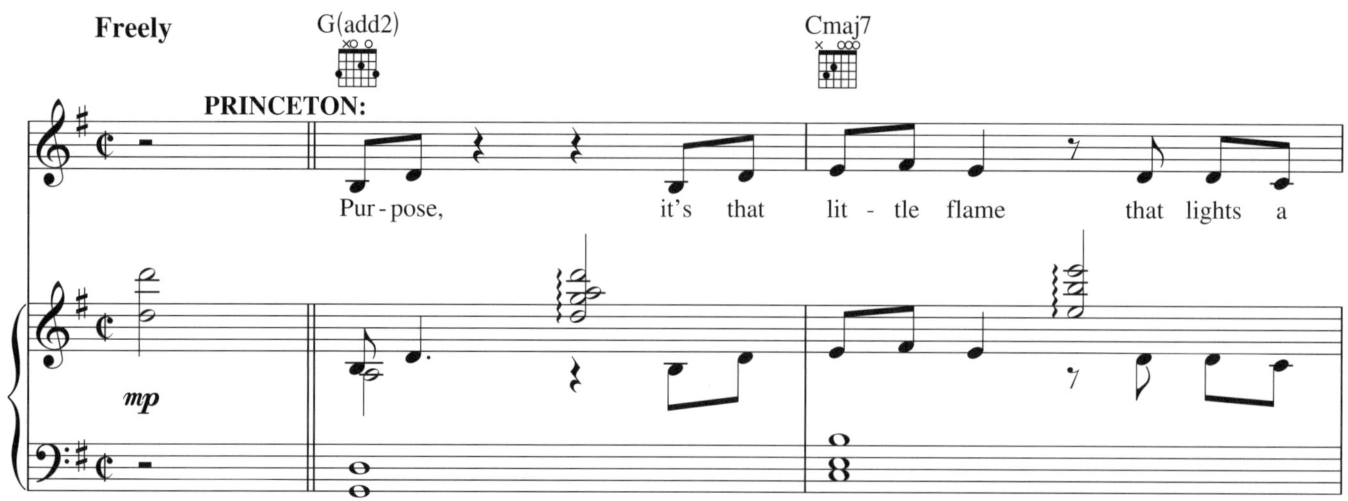

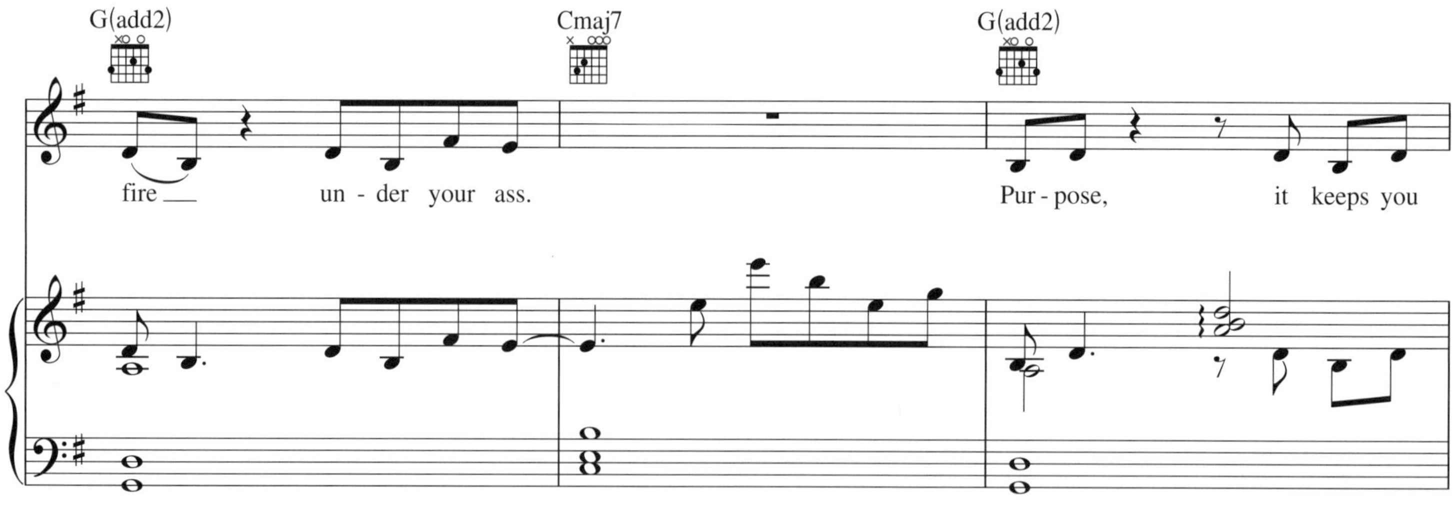

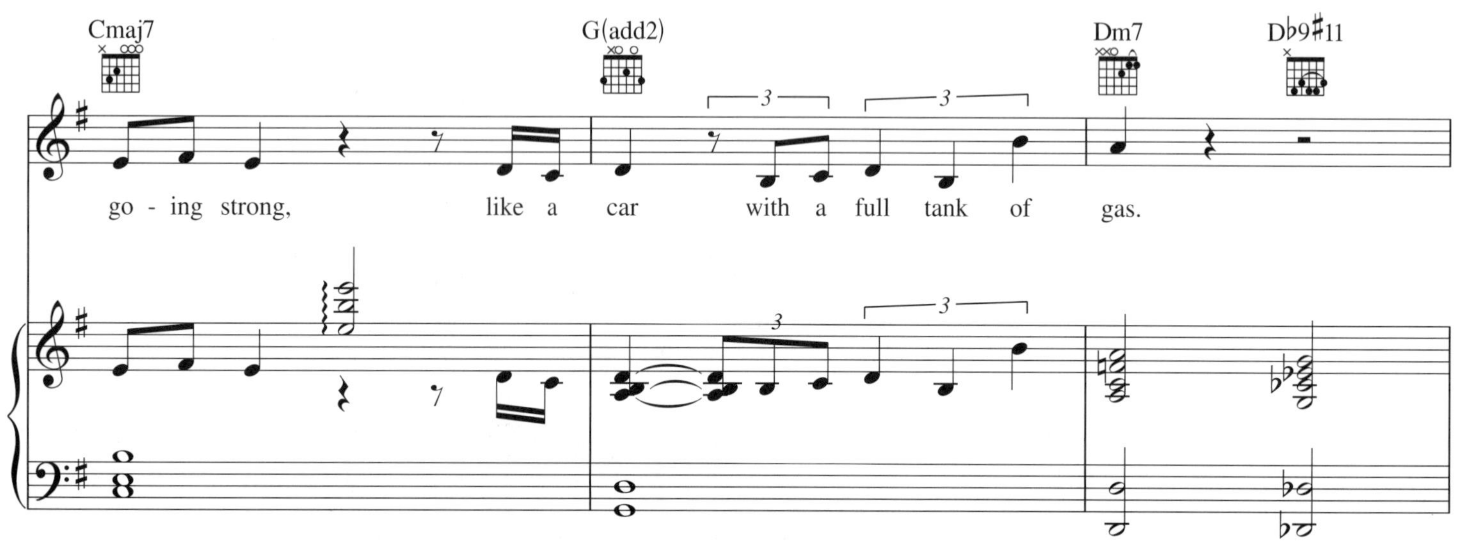

Cmaj7
Ev - 'ry - one else has a pur - pose. So, what's
Bm7 Em7 Asus A
mine? Hm. Oh, look: Here's a pen-ny! It's from the year I was born! It's a
a tempo
Tempo di "Huey Lewis" (Shuffle)
G/D D G
sign!
mf
D/E Em7 C(add2) G/D D G7sus/D D
Ba ba ba ba doo doo doo doo doo.

G(add2)
D/E
Em7
C(add2)
I don't know how I know, but I'm gonna
G/D
D
C/D
D
G(add2)
Bm7
Em7
find my pur-pose. I don't know where I'm gon-na look,
Am7
G/D
D
C/D
D
Half-time feel
Em
but I'm gon-na find my pur-pose. Got-ta find out.
D♯+
3fr
G/D
Em/C♯
Don't wan-na wait. Got to make sure that my life will be great!

Shuffle feel
Am7
G/B
C
Got-ta find my pur - pose before it's too late.
G(add2)
D/E
Em7
Whoa, whoa,
MOVING BOXES: (He's gon - na find his pur - pose.)
C(add2)
G/D
D
C/D
D
I'm gon - na find my pur - pose!

G(add2)
D/E
Em7
Yeah, yeah, yeah,
(He's gon - na find his pur - pose.)
C(add2)
G/D
D
C/D
D
I'm gon - na find my pur - pose!
Half-time feel
E
E/D
Cmaj7
Could be far, could be near. Could take a week, a
mp sub.

G/D
D
C/D
D
E
month, a year.
At a job,
E/D
Cmaj7
or smok - in' grass.
May - be at a
G/D
D
C/D
D
E
pot - ter - y class.
Could it be?
E/D
Cmaj7
Em/D
D
Em7/D
Yes, it could! Some - thin's com - in', some - thin' good!

Shuffle feel
G(add2)
D/E
Em7
C(add2)
G/D
D
Gsus/D
3fr
D
I'm gon - na find my pur - pose, yeah!
G(add2)
D/E
Em7
Whoa, whoa,
MOVING BOXES: (You're gon - na find your pur - pose.)
C(add2)
G/D
D
C/D
D
I'm gon - na find it!

Half-time feel
Em
Em(maj7)/D♯
What will it be? Where will it be? My
G/D
C♯m7♭5
4fr
pur - pose in life is a mys - ter - y!
Shuffle feel
Am7
G/B
Csus2
3fr
Got - ta find my pur - pose.
C5/D
G
Em7
D
Got-ta find me! Whoa, whoa,
(You're gon - na find your pur - pose!)

C(add2)
G/D
D
Gsus/D
3fr
G
I'm gon - na find my pur - pose!
D/E
Em7
D
C(add2)
C/D
D
Pur - pose! Pur - pose! Pur - pose! Yeah, yeah!
G5
3fr
I got - ta find me!

MAMA WHO BORE ME

from SPRING AWAKENING

Music by DUNCAN SHEIK
Lyrics by STEVEN SATER

Am
F(add2)/C
G(add2)/B
D(add2)
F(add2)
C(add2)/E
No sleep in Heav - en or Beth - le - hem.
Some pray that one day Christ
Dsus
D
F(add2)/C
G(add2)/B
Asus
A
will come a' call - ing.
They light a can - dle and hope that it glows.
F(add2)
C(add2)/E
Dsus
D
And some just lie there, cry - ing for Him to come and find them.
But
F(add2)/C
G(add2)/B
Asus
when He comes, they don't know how to go.
cresc.

A
F(add2)/C
G(add2)/B
D(add2)
Ma-ma, who bore me, Ma-ma, who gave me
mf
no way to han-dle things, who made me so bad.
Ma-ma, the weep-ing,
Ma-ma, the an-gels.
No sleep in Heav-en
G/B
Asus
or Beth-le-hem.
rit.

THE SONG THAT GOES LIKE THIS

from MONTY PYTHON'S SPAMALOT

C
F
C/E
A/C♯
LADY OF THE LAKE:
Where is it? Where? Where? A sen - ti-men-tal song that casts a mag-ic spell. They
Dm
Dm9/C
3fr
B♭
F
Dm
all will hum a-long. We'll o-ver-act like hell. Oh, this is the
Gm7
3fr
C7
F
B♭/F
DENNIS:
song that goes like this. Yes, it is!
F
B♭
LADY:
DENNIS:
LADY:
DENNIS:
Yes, it is! Yes, it is! Yes, it is!
3
Now we can go straight in -
cresc.
mf

F/A Gm7 C7 F F7/A
3fr
LADY:
to the mid-dle eight, a bridge that is too far for me. I'll
B♭ A7 Dm G7
BOTH:
sing it in your face, while we both em-brace, and then we change the
C D7 G
DENNIS: (opt. 8va)
key! Now we're in - to E. That's
cresc.
f
D/F♯ Em Em9/D C
LADY:
BOTH:
aw-fully high for me. But ev-'ry - one can see we should have stayed in D. For

G
Em
Am7
Dsus
this is our song that goes like this.
D
G
DENNIS:
I'm feel-ing ver-y proud.
LADY:
You're
D/F♯
Em
Em9/D
sing-ing far too loud.
DENNIS:
That's the way that this song goes.
LADY:
You're
C
G
Em
Am7
stand-ing on my toes.
BOTH:
Sing - ing our song that goes like

Dsus D Esus E

this. LADY: I

A E/G♯

DENNIS: LADY:

can't be - lieve there's more. It's far too long, I'm sure. That's the

F♯m F♯m7/E D

BOTH:

trou - ble with this song, it goes on and on and on. For

A F♯m Bm7 Esus E

DENNIS: LADY:

this is our song that is too long.

E/F♯
F♯
B
DENNIS:
LADY:
DENNIS:
Je - sus Christ! God damn it! We'll be sing-ing this till dawn. You'll
F♯/A♯
G♯m
G♯m9/F♯
LADY:
BOTH:
wish that you weren't born. Let's stop this damn re - frain, be -
E
B
G♯m
DENNIS:
LADY:
fore we go in - sane. The song al - ways
rit. poco a poco
C♯m7
F♯
F♯7
E/B
B
BOTH:
ends like this.
molto rit.
fff
All the glass on the chandelier breaks.

DECEMBER 1963
(Oh, What a Night)
featured in JERSEY BOYS

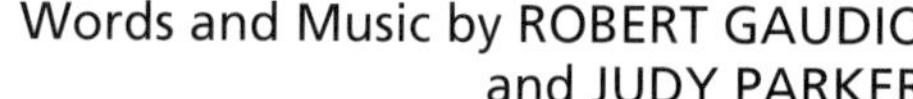

Moderate Rock

C F C/G F/G C F

f

F/G C F G7

Oh, what a night, late Decem - ber back in
night. You know, I did - n't e - ven
Hyp - no - tiz - in', mez-mer -
Instrumental solo
Why'd it take so long to

C F G C F

six - ty - three. What a ver - y spe - cial time for me, as
know her name, but I was nev - er gon - na be the same.
iz - ing me, she was ev - 'ry - thing I dreamed she'd be.
see the light? Seemed so wrong, but now it seems so right.

G
C
F
To Coda
I re - mem - ber, what a night.
What a la - dy, what a night.
Sweet sur - ren - der, what a night.
Instrumental ends
What a la - dy, what a night.
1
F/G
2
G
Dm
Oh, what a
Oh, I,
I
F
Fmaj7
Am
got a fun - ny feel - in' when she walked in the room.
G
Dm
Oh my, as

F
G6
I re - call, it end - ed much too soon.
C
1st time: D.S. al Coda
2nd time: D.S. al Coda
(take 2nd ending)
Oh, what a night!
CODA
F
G
Am
C
D
Dm7
Em7
I felt a rush like a roll - in' ball of thun - der,

F
1
G
D.S.S. (Instrumental)
(take 2nd ending)
spin - nin' my head a - round and tak - in' my bod - y un - der.
2
G
C
F
tak - in' my bod - y un - der.
G
C
F
Oh, what a night!
G
C
F
Repeat and Fade
Oh, what a night!